MOTHER MEERA

ANSWERS

Part II

Mother Meera
Oberdorf 4a
65599 Dornburg-Thalheim
Germany
Phone +49-(0)6436-91050, 91051
Fax +49-(0)6436-2361

ISBN 978-0-9802449-0-8

Copyright © 1997, 2008 Mother Meera

Printed in Canada

All rights reserved. No part of this book may be reproduced by any means without prior written permission from Mother Meera.

CONTENTS

Introduction 7
Paramatman..13
Avatars 15
Mother Meera and Mr. Reddy 19
Mother Meera 24
Darshan 36
The Divine and Man..46
Enlightenment and Realisation...............................52
Gurus 56
Japa and Meditation 60
Spiritual Life 67
Help and Grace 80
Karma and Past Lives..99
Astrology and Rituals 104
Channeling and Messages 109
Religion...113
Marriage and Family Life 116
Health and Medicine...134
Death and Suicide..143
Work..150
Food 156
The World...158
India 162
General 165

Sri Aurobindo Research Academy 179
Names and Terms 187
Darshan Information 192

Thalheim, Germany 1995

INTRODUCTION

An Avatar is an Incarnation of the Divine and comes to Earth whenever there is a need to uplift and protect humanity.

One of the most widely revered and loved of these Avatars is Mother Meera, a young Indian woman, born on December 26th, 1960, in the village of Chandepalle in Southern India. She soon showed Herself to be an unusual child. Her parents treated Her as exceptional and loved Her very much. The family was not especially religious and She was not brought up in any tradition. Her real parents were the spiritual guides that She met in vision, it was from them that She received the love and help She needed. Under the auspices of Her uncle, Mr. Reddy, She lived for some time in Pondicherry where Her extraordinary Presence attracted considerable attention. She is now worshipped as a Divine Mother all over India. In 1982 Mother Meera married a German who stays with Her in Thalheim, a quiet German village. Although She has not sought publicity thousands of people from both the East and the West recognise Mother Meera as Divine Mother and come to Her to receive Her Darshan, Her silent bestowal of Grace and Light through Her gaze and touch. No teachings, no rituals, no chanting, only Silent Blessings. Without spoken language Her inner Influence changes the hearts and minds of people. Simply being in Her presence gives the feeling of being in the Presence of the Supreme. Her gaze penetrates the soul, heart and mind. Silence expresses Her Beauty and majestic Power, Her Love and Purity.

In the company of Mother Meera I understand and feel and experience the different aspects of the Divine Mother. Her Personality, Her movements and Her Glance give a profound feeling of Sacred Love and Purity, each action is a quotation from the Gita, the Vedas or Bible. Her way of life is so simple both in words and action. As the sun cannot be separated from its brilliance, neither can Her Actions be separated from Her Words. The Mother is a practical example to us all that one can live in this world and at the same time be one with God.

It was my spiritual thirst for the Divine which led me first to Sri Aurobindo Ashram in Pondicherry and finally to the Mother. When I first met Her, She was thirteen years old. At first sight, I felt Her as the Divine Mother and experienced Her as Durga. Later I experienced Her aspect of Maheshwari in Her Wisdom, and witnessed the helping of people with problems by Her all-knowing advice. Business men, doctors, barristers, musicians, actors, architects have always been amazed by Her Knowledge. By Her Wisdom, Her explanations and logical analysis of daily life, She gradually changed my superstitious traditional beliefs and restored in their place light, love and knowledge. Still in India, the caste system exists along with "touchability" and "untouchability", but from childhood the Mother lived alongside differing castes and religions and says there is no difference between them. She does, however, understand that it is very difficult for human beings to accept cultures and religions other than their own. But for the Mother it was all quite simple.

In *Answers* we see Her full awareness of the world, Her understanding of the difficulties and sufferings and most practical solutions for the problems of everyday life, of different relationships, family life, work and also the spiritual life. We see Her Love for humanity, Her intense interest in the material and worldly welfare of people. Her Compassion is as vast as the ocean and She is so humble. Sometimes people not only called for help for themselves and their friends but also for their household pets.

My experience of the aspect of the Mother as Saraswati is seeing the perfection of Her work. From gardening to building construction She does all with exceptional patience and to the rhythm of Nature, and I marvel at the "Energy" which allows Her to work continuously without resting.

My knowledge of Her as an Avatar is quite special. Alone, if no help is available, Mother carries out construction work, laying bricks, building walls, climbing onto the roof. Recently at the new property the entire old roof had to be removed and a new one put on. In the Darshan Hall the roof had to be raised almost a metre, about three feet. During this time the Mother worked day and night without any rest, and as usual gave Darshan to devotees with the same intensity of Love and Peace. She has also worked on the insulation in the new building and watched over the whole operation with a constant vigilance, all with the same untiring rhythm. It is awe-inspiring to see and feel Her Divine Presence in action! At these times I feel strongly Her aspect as Mahakali.

Her fourth main aspect is Mahalakshmi, and there is no aspect more attractive to the heart of human beings. To be close to Her is profound happiness and to feel Her within the heart is a rapture. This we can experience during Darshan.

For almost twenty-six years I have been with the Mother and my knowledge is always being enhanced by hearing Her answers to people with widely differing personalities and professions. I feel deeply Her Love and Wisdom, as well as Her Care and Concern for each individual. Even though I have spent nearly half my life with Her, yet still She is a Divine Mystery.

- *Adilakshmi*

General Message

"Do your job and stay where you are. Pray to the Divine. I will help you."

- Mother Meera

PARAMATMAN

Question: Is Paramatman Light coming down now?

Mother Meera: The Light is continuously coming down. Some see it already at Darshan. Some see it outside Darshan. Eventually everyone will see it and be transformed.

Q: If Paramatman is the Supreme God, is it necessary to pray to other Gods like Brahma, Vishnu, Shiva, Durga etc.?

MM: Yes, if you want you can pray to any God you believe in.

Q: How do we feel the difference between the Supramental Light and Paramatman Light?

MM: The Supramental Light can burn slightly when you receive it. The Supreme Light does not hurt.

Q: What is the difference between Paramatman Light and Supramental Light.

MM: All Lights come from Paramatman Light.

Q: OM is everything and everything came from it. What is the relation between OM and Paramatman?

MM: OM is a manmade word to describe creation. Everything came from Paramatman.

Q: Please describe Paramatman.

MM: Paramatman is the origin, the essence of the entire universe. There is no place without it but it has no name or form.

Q: Is Paramatman masculine or feminine?

MM: Paramatman has no form or gender.

Q: What is the relationship of Adiparashakti to Paramatman?

MM: Paramatman is Supreme. All comes from Paramatman.

Q: What is the difference between light particles or light waves measured by scientific analysis and the Paramatman light?

MM: The light of the sun is hot but the Paramatman Light is cool and contains all the other lights.

AVATARS

Q: Ma, are you in contact with Avatars and can you speak to them?

MM: Yes.

Q: Do you like being Mother Meera?

MM: There is no liking or disliking. I came for that and I am that.

Q: Ma, after some years, even though your body is not on the earth, will your Power still be here?

MM: Present physically or not, the power of the Avatars is always present.

Q: What do you think of Gandhi? Was he an Avatar?

MM: No. He was a Vibhuti. He was a freedom fighter. He sacrificed his life for his country. Gandhi, Nehru and Indira Gandhi, all these people came for a special purpose.

Q: What is the difference between an Avatar and a Vibhuti?

MM: An Avatar is a divine incarnation and comes for the uplifting of the whole human race, for a divine purpose. A Vibhuti comes for a certain, specific work, more related to the world. For example, a politician could be a Vibhuti, like Mahatma Gandhi, Indira Gandhi etc.

Q: Is Vivekananda an Avatar?

MM: He was a messenger from God.

Q: I believe that Jesus Christ is not God, but he loves humanity. He is a lover of humanity.

MM: One judges according to one's knowledge and experience.

Q: I feel that Jesus is greater than Mary.

MM: You can believe according to your faith, but both have different functions. They came for different purposes. We cannot judge that one is greater than the other.

Q: Christ is the son of God but many devote themselves to the Virgin Mary.

MM: Both are symbolic of Love and Action. Both are great. Greatness cannot be explained in words.

Q: I think that an Avatar is more like a Mother than a Father.

MM: An Avatar is above both. An Avatar is Shakti itself.

Q: What is Shakti?

MM: With divine Shakti, we can do any work. If we have physical energy, we can do physical work well.

Q: Is Mary pre-eminent at this time?

MM: Divine is permanent at all times.

Q: Have Avatars incarnated before as human beings?

MM: Avatars come from Paramatman. To come to earth, they do not need to have previous incarnations as human beings. They are always Avatars. Whenever Paramatman asks them to go to earth, they are born on earth. Avatars have no good or bad karma. There is no karma for them. They are above karma. Karma is only for human beings.

Q: Can all Avatars see Paramatman?

MM: All Avatars can see Paramatman. Their way is different but the experience is the same.

Q: Did Krishna historically exist? If he existed, was he the same as described in the scriptures?

MM: Yes.

Q: Did Buddha ever do japa?

MM: He was more inside in himself, he was withdrawn within himself.

Q: What is the difference between an Avatar and a jnani?

MM: An Avatar is born with wisdom and a jnani achieves wisdom through sadhana.

MOTHER MEERA AND MR. REDDY

(Adilakshmi:) When I first heard about the Mother through Mr. Reddy in 1972 I felt that I knew Her. I had been searching for this Divine Mother. Mr. Reddy narrated to me how he met Mother and told me that he searched for this Mother for nearly 40 years. Once I asked the Mother how and where She met Mr. Reddy and what impressions She had about him. The Mother told me that even when She was a child, many times She had a vision of a man with a white dhoti and kurta (Indian man's dress) with a Gandhi cap. He was Mr. Reddy and She knew that he was going to play a very vital role in Her life. When She met Mr. Reddy near the bus stop in Her village, She recognised that he was the man in Her visions. I asked the Mother the following:

Adilakshmi: Dear Mother, when did you meet Mr. Reddy?

MM: When Mr. Reddy came from the ashram in Pondicherry to visit my village, I went to receive Mr. Reddy at the bus stop. One of his family members accompanied me to receive him. I was 12 years old.

Adilakshmi: What was Mr. Reddy's reaction?

MM: Mr. Reddy handed his suitcase to me. Then he asked, "Who is this girl?" Mr. Reddy stood on the first step of the bus, holding the rail ready to get down, but he was transfixed, with awareness and love.

(Adilakshmi:) The members of Mr. Reddy's family questioned the Divinity of the Mother. One day Mr. Reddy took Mother to Hyderabad and then returned to Chandepalle. There he had an experience of "seeing" the Mother in Chandepalle although she had remained in Hyderabad. Mr. Reddy narrated this story to me as follows: "I was sleeping at home in Chandepalle. I heard Mother calling me, 'Uncle!'. I awoke and saw Mother so vividly. Mother sat on a chair and I offered her a sweet dish (payasam). She ate it and spoke to me. Then she disappeared and I searched but could not find her. I later asked her if she had been in Chandepalle. She said she had remained in Hyderabad. I asked, 'Then how did you come?'"

"Mother explained to me, 'Physically, like for you, it is not necessary for me to come to see what is happening. If you concentrate and want to know what I am doing you can also see me. From now onwards, I will come to you many times. You should not worry about me but simply concentrate, then you can see what I am doing.'"

Once Mother stayed with friends of Mr. Reddy for several weeks. The couple had been married for a long time, but they didn't have any children. Soon after Mother came, the wife became pregnant. The wife said, "You came to my house and blessed me with a child."

Babu, Mother, Mr. Reddy and Adilakshmi 1984

For some months, Mother stayed with different friends of Mr. Reddy. All of these families looked after her with love. In 1974, she came to Pondicherry.

Knowing Mr. Reddy and his relationship with the Mother, many times I thought of the comparison of Lord Krishna, Yashoda and Nanda. Mr. Reddy, like Vasudeva (the father of Krishna) tried in many places to find parents for the Mother like Krishna's parents. Finally, Mr. Reddy decided to take the responsibility for the Mother both as a mother and father. He bid farewell to his family and property.

His first priority was the Mother. From that moment to the end of his life, he kept his promise and never left the Mother. Mr. Reddy travelled with the Mother to many places and many people who saw the Mother recognised her Divinity. Many of those who at first did not recognise her Divinity, later became devoted believers.

MOTHER MEERA

Q: Ma, some people call you a Guru, others call you an Avatar and still others Divine Mother. But really who are you?

MM: I came to help and save people who are in need.

Q: Have you had previous lives?

MM: Whenever there is necessity in the world and when the people need protection and help, I am there always.

Q: Have you always known who you are from birth?

MM: Yes, I have known who I am from birth. There has never been any separation between me and the Divine.

Q: I want to devote my life to you, Mother, what should I do?

MM: It is not necessary to devote your life to me or even believe in me. If you are sincere to your Guru, to your master and to God or to the Divine, it is enough and I will strengthen your faith. Finally, if you believe in God, that is enough for me. I suggest that you do your job and your duties wholeheartedly and joyfully and bring peace and happiness to your family and in your surroundings; do japa, the chanting or repeating of the name of God or whatever you believe in, and ask for whatever you want.

If you need me or my help I will help you whatever path you may follow. For me there is no difference. All paths lead to the same goal, that is, to realise the Divine.

Q: That means you never encourage us to leave our jobs, families, or countries?

MM: Yes. That is true. I suggest that people stay where they are. If they need help, I will help them. The help will come regardless of distance.

Q: Now you are living in Germany. Is there a special reason why you live in Europe?

MM: Yes.

Q: Why?

Adilakshmi: There are some special reasons and other practical reasons to stay in Germany, for example the dialysis for Mr Reddy.

Mother works silently. If human beings or any other beings in the whole universe recognise Her work or not, it does not matter for the Mother. The

Mother works constantly with patience. If we feel and are conscious of Her work, we will enjoy the beauty of the work. Trying to see Her way of action gives us real happiness and it will be deeply rooted in our hearts.

Q: Is Mother Meera Mother for other beings in the universe?

MM: Yes.

Q: Is your function as a Mother limited only to earth?

MM: No. Not only with the earth but also with other planets and other worlds, too.

Q: Are you involved in the guidance of beings, such as angels and devas, in order to develop this planet?

MM: Yes.

> (Adilakshmi:) On Mother's birthday someone brought a present and the Mother was starting to open it. The person asked the Mother if she already knew what was in it, and why open it? Mother said: "The other people present do not know."

Q: Can human beings follow your path, or is their path different? What are the essential steps human beings should take to contribute to the mission to transform the earth?

MM: All human beings can follow the same path. Remember the Divine or God always.

Q: During Darshan I received an image which reminds me of the large wings of the Egyptian Goddess Isis, Goddess of Fertility and linked with the Moon and Earth. Is Your function comparable with that of Isis?

MM: Yes.

Q: How does Paramatman Light affect you? What difference do you feel between Paramatman Light and the world?

MM: I do not feel any difference of it being present or not present. It is part of my body so I feel nothing special.

Q: Many of us open ourselves to you when we come to Darshan, then we feel anger after being immersed in bliss. Why?

MM: When you are far away, you have aspiration. When you come to Darshan and are filled with the Divine, then other qualities like anger, jealousy etc. arise because after an experience of the Divine, you become more conscious of your human qualities.

Q: I was in Auroville. Now I want to live in Germany. I want to live near you and find a job.

MM: Wherever you find a job there you can live. You do not have to live in Germany.

Q: Have you incarnated in the past?

MM: It is not important if I incarnated in the past or will incarnate in the future. The most and only important thing is that I am here now.

Q: Each Guru or each religion has their own way and they teach people to follow only their path, not any other way. You on the contrary allow all religions and all sects to follow their own way instead of your way. Why?

MM: To follow me there is no special rule. People can follow what they like. I will still help them all.

Q: Do the people who are living in your house believe only in you?

MM: No. They have their own way of faith. Some believe in Sri Aurobindo, some do TM (Transcendental Meditation), some have followed Rajneesh and some believe only in me. They can believe what they like. For me there is no difference. All rivers flow to the sea.

Q: Ma, do you think the people who are living with you and also people who are coming to you will stay permanently?

MM: I do not think so. It depends on them.

Q: Now huge numbers of people are coming to see you. Some have as their only aim and goal in their lives to be with you permanently.

MM: Generally, I do not encourage people to stay with me. They can live where they are. Their faith will grow when they have sincere aspiration. Then there is no difference between staying with me or being thousands of miles away.

Q: Why are you not charging money for Darshan?

MM: I do not like to charge in the name of the Divine. If people want to offer sincerely and wholeheartedly, they can offer what they want to give.

> (Adilakshmi:) Sometimes the Mother asks my opinions or my feelings. Once the Mother asked:

MM: For twenty years this person has had great love for two diamond rings and now she offers them to me. What is your opinion about her giving nature?

Adilakshmi: Mother! Are you asking me?

MM: Yes.

Adilakshmi: I feel that by giving without thinking of her physical security she surrenders to you, having full confidence in the Divine that the Divine will take care of her and that Divine security is real security.

> (Adilakshmi:) The Mother blessed the rings and returned them to the owner. When I returned them to the owner she was spellbound and tears ran down with joy and gratitude.

Q: How do you feel about the responsibility of being Mother Meera? Is it heavy on your shoulders?

MM: No.

Q: Do you think about yourself as Kamala Reddy or Mother Meera?

MM: I never think about it.

Q: How do you feel now that you are famous and many thousands of people are coming to see you?

MM: Human beings will feel great when they become famous but for me there is no difference.

Q: Why don't you feel any difference?

MM: Every human being has an ego. It is better not to give so much importance to the ego or to name and fame. Try to know that Paramatman is the greatest, then there is no ego.

Q: A famous Hollywood star came for Darshan. Did you know that he was coming to Darshan?

MM: Yes.

Q: When you go into the dreams of people, do you know it?

MM: No.

Q: Did you see the Olympics?

MM: No.

Q: Did any special events occur in the world when you were born?

MM: I do not know. People around me may know.

Q: Have any people reported significant events at your birth?

MM: I have never asked.

Q: Why were you born in that particular family in India?

MM: I was born there because of their aspiration.

Q: Do you speak with angels? If so, in which language?

MM: Yes. Soul has no language.

Q: Do you watch television? If so, what films do you like?

MM: Comedies.

Q: Recently, what comedy did you see?

MM: Terence Hill.

Q: What do you think about him.

MM: He is humble and simple like a child.

Q: Do you see Paramatman always?

MM: When I need, I see.

Q: How can you be sitting here with us and at the same time be in many other places?

MM: You are sitting here and your thoughts go in many places.

Q: Can you see the auras, i.e. the external energy fields?

MM: Yes.

Q: How can I know that you are Divine Mother?

MM: When you have some problem, then pray sincerely and ask for help.

Q: I saw you as Mother Durga. My friend wants to decorate you like that and wants to photograph you. I am an artist.

MM: By simply wearing a crown, one cannot become a Goddess, and by merely wearing a dhoti (Indian dress) you are not an Indian.

Q: Will you come back to the earth?

MM: No.

Q: Did you feel any burden on your shoulders when you came to the earth?

MM: There is not any burden. It is not necessary to come again and again.

Q: Will Mr. Reddy come back?

MM: No.

Q: Mother, I am very attracted to you. Don't I have to overcome this attachment?

MM: If you didn't feel attracted, you couldn't stay near me.

Q: We will bear all the expenses and also arrange for you and some of your devotees to visit each country and each state. Why do you not accept our invitation?

MM: At this moment, I don't like to travel. Being two days here, four days there and six days in some other place is like a carnival or festival.

Q: I came to know you through my employer but now I am not working for him. Have you left me?

Adilakshmi: The Divine Mother is for all mankind. The Divine is always with sincere and loving people. Wherever we may be, in whatever condition we may be in, the Mother is always with us. You must not think that the Mother will not be with you if you leave your job. Everyone has his or her own relationship with the Divine. We can meet or know the Divine through any one. That is not important. Each individual has a direct contact with the Divine. The Mother's Love is above all human relations. The Mother is with you wherever you may be. You must be free from doubt. Have confidence in the Mother, the Mother's help and blessings will always be there. You can write letters and have the contact as before.

Q: What do you think about your neighbours?

MM: All neighbours should be healthy, happy and should not have any suffering.

Q: Do you love all people in the same way?

MM: I love all mankind in the same way. But if they are cunning, hypocritical and not straightforward, I do not like these qualities. I do not tell people that they have such qualities. The light awakens them to all other qualities.

Q: Some people are good and some people are bad. Do you judge them?

MM: No. Good and bad are relative.

DARSHAN

(Adilakshmi:) Mr. Reddy used to say that he knew different kinds of great personalities and avadhutas like Chinnamma, Dontulamma, yogis like Ramananda, Manikyamma, divine personalities like Sweet Mother and Satya Sai Baba. He found that the Mother's way of pranam and Darshan is completely different from others. He also asked the scholars of Sanskrit and also well versed Veda Pundits if this method of pranam and Darshan exists in the scriptures. They informed him that they did not find this type of Darshan.

Q: Mother, do you have any special preparations before Darshan?

MM: No.

Q: What do you do after Darshan?

MM: Nothing special.

Q: Are you tired after Darshan?

MM: No.

Q: Do you like to give Darshan?

MM: Yes.

Q: You have been giving Darshan for 25 years. Are you not tired?

MM: No.

Q: During Darshan, people kneel down before you. How do you feel about it?

MM: For me that has no special importance. People come because of their need. If they have devotion in their life, I receive it with tenderness and love.

Q: Why do people kneel?

MM: If they do not kneel, I cannot reach to touch their head.

Q: When you first start to touch the head of a person, how do you feel?

MM: They will feel something but I do not feel anything.

Q: Is your method a new way of giving Darshan?

MM: Yes.

Q: Who teaches this method?

MM: No one. This is my way.

Q: What do you see in their eyes?

MM: I see many things and help them to solve their problems.

Q: If you know a person's problem, why don't you talk to them about it?

MM: I do not like to hurt or praise people by saying that they have this or that problem. If they have a problem, in silence I will help them. This is my way.

Q: Is it true that one can receive more in silence?

MM: Yes. When you are in silence, there are less thoughts and you can see clearly what your problem is, where to focus, where the problem lies, how to get rid of it or who is really responsible, how much oneself is involved in it and so on. If you want to solve it with a calm mind you find the solution and when you pray, you also receive the solution to your problem.

Q: What is the best attitude towards Darshan?

MM: People can come for Darshan with an open mind and freely. But they should not impose any conditions on the Mother. For example, people ask if she is married or ill or has children. We must be free from all such mental constructions.

Q: Some people are satisfied with one Darshan and some are never satisfied. Why?

MM: Some are never satisfied because they are inwardly restless and have no patience. It is in their nature to never feel satisfied within themselves.

Q: When you touch the head, you see the white and red lines. Are they inside the body or outside the body?

MM: Inside the body.

Q: When do you stop Darshan?

MM: It depends on me.

Q: Do different people have different experiences during Darshan?

MM: Yes.

Q: Does the same person always have the same experience in Darshan?

MM: No, it is different.

Q: Some people say that when you touch our head, it is not scientifically possible to give such energy within such a short time.

MM: If you read the Puranas, the Vedas and other scriptures, there are examples that within a fraction of a second one can realise God. Science will come to understand energy, as the consciousness of scientists expands. Specifically, if a scientist receives the light, his understanding of the energy will grow.

Q: What should my attitude be towards the energy I receive from you?

MM: The energy or the Light which you receive in Darshan acts in its own way. It works in its own way. There is nothing for you to do. There are no specific laws or rules or regulations to follow. But you can pray and do japa and ask for the right attitude. The right attitude opens the mind and heart so true understanding and true feelings grow.

Q: I am coming from very far away, from Australia. I want to see your smile and hear your voice.

MM: I give Darshan in silence. If you want to come and have Darshan in silence it is OK. To hug or hear my voice or see my smile is not my way. Please do not repeatedly request things that are not my way.

Q: I have been coming to Darshan for many years. I originally approached Mother with an open but very intellectually analytical mind. Now I feel overwhelming love, that I never felt before in my life. But even on the physical level, I think that the Mother is not human but

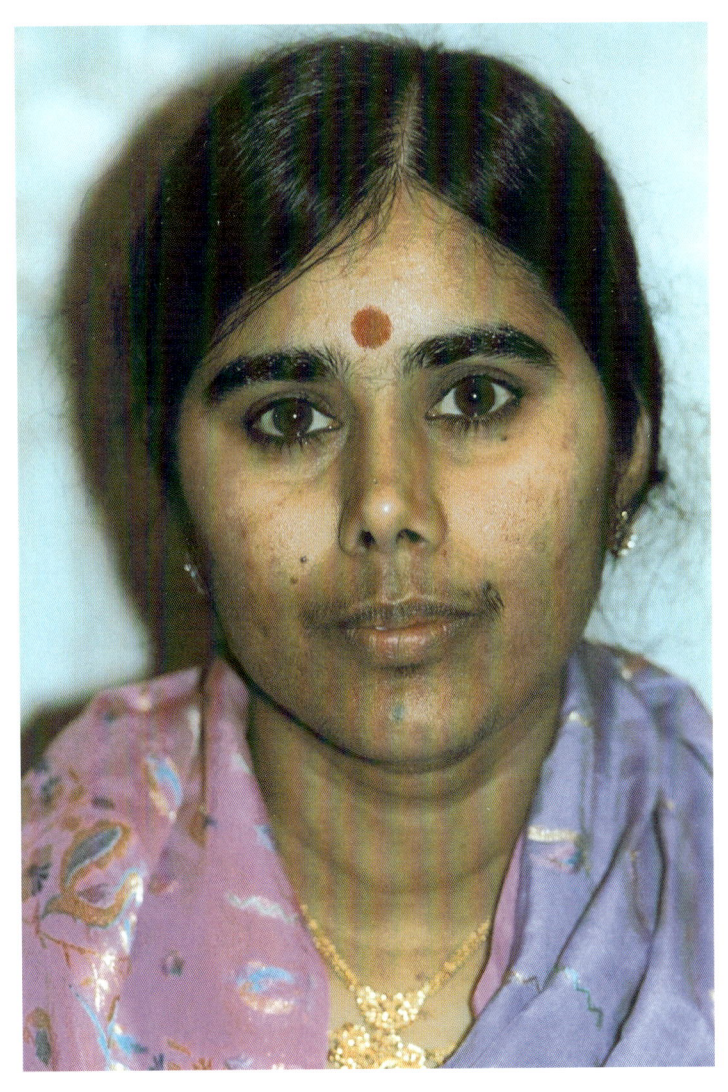

Thalheim, Germany 1995

divine. During Darshan, the Mother is fully and equally concentrated on each person. Mother spends two to three hours, four days a week, year after year giving Darshan. In my experience it is not possible for a human being to have such constant concentration. Is this true?

Adilakshmi: It is true. Her patience and concentration are like a majestic mountain.

Q: Is the Mother courageous and strong during Darshan?

Adilakshmi: The Mother is very courageous, strong and gracious. Nearly four hundred eyes focus on Her during Darshan but She is always calm, still and unchanging.

Q: During Darshan, when we receive Mother's Light, sometimes we see more darkness within ourselves. One is horrified to see this falsehood within oneself with such clarity. What should we do?

MM: Be calm and offer it to the Divine.

Q: People have come to you for Darshan from all over the world and yet for the most part since you came to Europe you have remained in a small village in a quiet corner of Germany. What made you decide to remain here when so many others who have offered spiritual help often travelled the world in a very public and visible way?

MM: In my way, in order to help people, it is not necessary to travel. Regardless of where people live, if they need my help, if they pray sincerely and wholeheartedly, they will get my help regardless of my physical separation.

Q: Can you tell us briefly what Darshan involves and why it is helpful to those who come to you.

MM: People come to Darshan to have their own experience.

> (Adilakshmi:) A seven year old American child came to Darshan for the first time. After Darshan I asked him, "How is Darshan?" Poetically he replied, "Mother's eyes are crystals cleansing the soul." This expression of truth touched my heart. This is wonderful to feel. His answer is simple. His love for the Mother is great. He wants to build a castle, where there will be a very big hall only for Mother's Darshan. His love for the Mother made me happy. He is a great soul. Children are more open to the Divine and it is easy for them to feel the Divine Presence. I told the Mother the beautiful experience of the child. The Mother listened silently and nodded her head.
>
> I asked one of the first time visitors to Darshan, whose mother had previously been to Darshan, about her experience. She said that it is a miracle that her

mother, a conservative Catholic, had a profound experience with the Mother. So she decided to come and see the Mother herself. "Darshan was very powerful for both of us. My mother is now experiencing the Divine Mother's Grace very strongly in her life as well. I cannot express my gratitude for this experience. Before, my mother and I did not have a good relationship but now it is completely changed. I want to say that there began a period of deep peace, happiness, and closeness with the Divine. My life had always been pretty intense and dramatic until then. This profound peace and inner connection became pretty steady in the background of my activities. Through these experiences I truly learned to love and trust the Mother. The best way I can describe Darshan is that it feels like I swallowed a piece of the Sun and every part of my being, every cell is basking in its warm, radiant light."

అమ్మ

THE DIVINE AND MAN

Q: You have said, "When you know you are Divine, you can become completely human." What does it mean?

MM: The Divine can come to the human level and the human can understand completely his relationship with the Divine.

Q: Will the Divine destroy all of humanity?

MM: No, the Divine does not destroy, human beings destroy.

Q: In the scriptures I read that with the permission of Adiparashakti birth and death takes place. Is this true?

MM: Yes.

Q: Advaita describes that the world is an illusion. Is this true?

MM: The world is real because we touch, feel, see and we live in it. One can say that God is an illusion, if one doesn't have any connection with Him. If you have the connection, you may understand that God is real but not the world.

Q: What is the best way for people to discover their life's purpose at this time?

MM: At this time or at any time the purpose of the human being is to remember the Divine.

Q: If people want to know their life's purpose but do not know Mother Meera, is your energy available to help those persons to discover their purpose?

MM: It is not necessary to know me. If people are sincere and faithful to their faith whatever path or religion or technique it may be, I help them to find out their purpose and also strengthen their faith.

Q: Why would God ask us to love Him?

MM: God never comes and asks us to love Him. Human beings themselves create the temples and forms of worship because they want to experience God's love. Avatars come to earth because of God's love and human beings experience the greatness of love in the Avatars.

Q: Is it possible for a person to receive the Light at all times?

MM: No.

Q: Why?

MM: Man has a physical life, a mental life, and a spiritual life. It is generally impossible for man to be always in the spiritual life. For some people the physical life dominates and for others the mental life or the spiritual life dominates. It is possible to open only sometimes to the Light.

Q: Is it true that everyone has light?

MM: If everyone has light, then there is no suffering.

Q: Does Mother Meera know who I am?

MM: It is not necessary to know who you are but it is better for you to know who I am.

Q: Sometimes I think that the Divine is selfish. Is it true?

MM: No, the Divine is selfless. You come to the Divine and you receive peace, happiness and satisfy yourself. You are not giving anything to the Divine. After satisfying yourself, you go away. After some years, when your desires are not fulfilled, you blame the Divine. In the end what you have given to the Divine is only selfishness. Even if you bow down to the Divine, you do it with an expectation of something from the Divine with selfish motive, not with unselfishness.

Q: Is it true that if we hurt human beings, we hurt Paramatman?

MM: It is not true.

Q: People praise Premamayi (Ocean of Love), Karunamayi (Epitome of Compassion), Divine Mother and so on when something good happens but if even a small desire of theirs is not fulfilled the same person blames the Mother. Why is this?

MM: Because of their ignorance and also because they don't have deep enough devotion and faith.

Q: My time in life is precious. Should I spend my time searching for God?

MM: Your time is not precious. Divine time is precious.

Q: I have spent many hours working for the Divine.

MM: When we work for the Divine, count not the hours.

Q: I am peaceful and happy in your presence. Is my experience true or false?

MM: I do not decide if your experience is true or false. When you hear something against your Guru or Avatar or master, if you are not shaken by hearing that, then your experience is true.

Q: What is the difference between human and Divine?

MM: It is the law that the human has to change in order to unite with the Divine.

Q: I am feeling guilty and I am miserable. What shall I do?

MM: Offer your feeling of guilt to God or the Divine. You can follow your own path. I will help you.

Q: Many people seem to go through a pattern of believing in the Divine and praising the Divine but later on they turn against the Divine and even blame the Divine. Why do people change?

MM: For example, if you go shopping and after searching for a particular dress, you find one matching your taste, you buy it. Every day you wear it. After a while, you throw it away because it is old. In the same way, you come to the Divine. You search for the Divine here and there until you find the Divine. You are satisfied and content and you praise the Divine. Day after day, as long as you are satisfied you stay loyal and praise. Later on, when small desires of the ego are not fulfilled, your ego blames the Divine. As you throw away the old dress, in the same manner you reject the Divine. You paid money to have a dress you loved but then rejected it. Similarly, most people try to use the Divine and then reject it.

But the Divine is always the same, eternal and full. It is like an ocean, never ending. Many come with thirst. According to their thirst, they drink and their thirst is fulfilled. But the ocean is always full and never empty. Man, after satisfying his thirst, completely forgets God. Instead of being grateful, he is ungrateful. This is human nature. This is where man must change.

Q: If someone writes negatively about the Divine, what is your reaction? Does it hurt you?

MM: The position of the Divine does not change. For a famous man, when something bad is known to the public, it damages his fame. But the Divine's position is eternal. If someone writes something bad about the Divine, it effects only the writer, a friend of the writer or some of his relatives or persons who accept the writing, not everybody. If your faith is not strong then it effects you and doubt will dominate.

అమ్మ

ENLIGHTENMENT AND REALISATION

Q: Are you enlightened?

MM: Enlightenment is only for human beings. Avatars give the enlightenment to human beings. Avatars are born enlightened.

Q: Can a sincere disciple who dedicates his life to God expect salvation? Can you hasten the process of incarnations?

MM: You can dedicate your life and be sincere but do not expect salvation. It always takes its own time.

Q: A friend who has cancer went to Benares to die. Is it true that if one dies there one gets liberation?

MM: That depends on one's sincere aspiration and God's grace.

Q: What is enlightenment?

MM: There are no words to describe it. One can only experience it. Union with the Divine or Paramatman is an experience.

Q: Is enlightenment possible for everyone?

MM: Yes.

Q: What are the essential qualities one must have to be enlightened?

MM: First do your job or work or profession perfectly. Have a strong will, aspiration, and devotion.

Q: Why do we need enlightenment?

MM: We need enlightenment to be free from our daily problems, to rise from suffering to bliss, from ignorance to wisdom, from darkness to light, from mortality to immortality.

Q: In ancient India, the saints have experienced jivan-mukti. Mother, could you kindly give me mentally the experience even for a fraction of a second?

MM: When this is experienced, there is no mind, the experience is union with the Divine.

Q: Do you believe that X who is living, is realised?

MM: Realisation is only after death.

Q: What about people like Ramana Maharshi, who experienced death and was reborn again?

MM: There are so many deaths on the path, death of ego etc.

Q: Mother! Even if you say that realisation is not for me in this life, I will always desire it.

MM: If you are sincere and surrender to the Divine completely, then it is possible.

Q: I am a householder. My family is good, happy and harmonious. I want to realise God.

MM: People put too much emphasis on realisation. In my view, it will take lifetimes. Instead, it is better to love and remember the Divine.

Q: When will the world be enlightened?

MM: When there is no difference between rich and poor, no caste, no different religions, no colour difference, no different nationalities, no differences among human beings, then there will be enlightenment.

Q: Can I become enlightened?

MM: When we have jealousy, anger, selfishness, then it is not possible.

Q: Is it true that we can get realisation by paying money and by sitting daily for some hours in meditation?

MM: Yogis should not meditate for realisation but for Paramatman's Darshan.

Q: There are teachers in the West nowadays who say that realisation or enlightenment are not far from us and that they can be reached right away. Is that so?

MM: No.

Q: Osho says, that one cannot do anything by oneself for realisation.

MM: It depends on God's grace and also on your sincere aspiration.

Q: Mother, is it possible to be enlightened without leaving the active world? Or should one go into a cave?

MM: Nowadays not even Gurus are going into caves.

అమ్మ

GURUS

Q: Is it possible to have a Guru and disciple relationship with a living Guru if the Guru and disciple live apart?

MM: It is not possible if the Guru lives in one place and the disciple lives in another. If the disciple lives with the Guru and serves and surrenders without having any personal life, then it is possible to have that kind of traditional relationship. At this time, it is not necessary to have that kind of relationship to reach God. It is helpful, but true aspiration, sincerity and love will lead you to God.

Q: I am a Sufi. I have no living master. I would like to have one.

MM: If you have confidence in your faith, it is not necessary to have a living Guru.

Q: Many Gurus are saying that they are enlightened.

MM: If they are enlightened then it is not necessary for them to live in the world.

Q: My Guru told me that I must follow only his way and not come to you.

MM: God is one. You will stay with your Guru until your destiny or your fate or until your karma causes you to leave. When the time is over, even if he says that you must believe only in him and not in others, you cannot stay with him. If your heart sincerely tells you to stay with him, you will stay.

Q: How do we determine whether a Guru is legitimate? For example, someone was worshipped as a Guru but later he was in jail. Is he a fake?

MM: We cannot consider a person to be a fake simply because he went to jail. Jail is not necessarily the criteria to judge if he is good or bad. Sri Aurobindo went to jail.

Q: Will you comment about Ammachi or Gurumayi?

Adilakshmi: Generally the Mother doesn't give comments like that.

Q: How can we differentiate between Gurus and Avatars?

MM: According to your experience, you can differentiate between them.

Q: Why should a Guru have the rule that the disciples must believe only in him and not in other Gurus and also that they must stay in the ashram and not visit other Gurus or Avatars?

MM: Human beings frequently change their minds. For example when some were young, they believed in Jesus or Mary, then they joined the TM movement, after that they believed in Sai Baba. Now they believe in me and tomorrow they believe in something else. Because people go on changing from one Guru to another, the Guru makes the rule that it is better for the disciple to stay where he is and not visit others.

Q: But you are accepting all and you are giving us a chance to experience different kinds of Gurus, sects and religions.

MM: I am not a Guru.

Q: Is it possible for the Guru to take away the karma and diseases of the disciple. Is it possible for the Guru to get the illness of the disciples?

MM: If the disciples are not completely surrendered, the Gurus do not get the illness of the disciples. When the disciple helplessly and completely surrenders to the Guru, then the Guru will take the whole responsibility for the disciple. When a helpless child completely depends on the mother, then the mother will take complete responsibility to fulfil the child's wish.

Q: I want to visit an Avatar and also some other realised Gurus but I am busy. Is it good to do so?

MM: If you want to go and visit the Divine with devotion and a pure heart, with selfless motive, then you will get something. With a selfish motive if you visit, you cannot get anything.

Q: For 20 years, I have been a devotee of a well-known Master. Now, I feel that I want to offer my devotion to another Guru. What shall I do?

MM: Nowadays, you can change your guru. I don't see any problem in that.

అమ్మ

JAPA AND MEDITATION

Q: In the past I experienced light and ananda but now I feel empty. Should I practice more meditation?

MM: Not more practice but stronger aspiration.

Q: What is japa?

MM: Japa is one way to remember God.

Q: Is it necessary to have a mantra for japa?

MM: No. Instead of a mantra, you can repeat one word or the two letters "Ma" or "Amma". This is enough. If you do not pronounce the mantra properly then the results will be bad. So it is better to do japa with simple words which come spontaneously from the heart.

Q: Is it possible for a person who can sit quietly in a still position for a long time to receive the Supramental light based on the stillness alone?

MM: No.

Q: Is it good to talk about You.

Adilakshmi: Yes. When we talk about the Mother, the vibrations of the Mother will spread. When we talk about the Mother with so much love, the love itself creates a beautiful, soft, and pleasant atmosphere and people feel this shift in the atmosphere, lightness rather than heaviness. It is also a kind of japa that we are remembering the Divine. It is a good opportunity for the speaker and the listener.

Q: I sit and meditate many hours to get light. When shall I get the light?

MM: It is not necessary to sit and meditate many hours to get light. The light will come in its own way. One has to practice one's path regularly without worrying about the result. The light occurs spontaneously, like the blossoming of a flower.

Q: How can I tell my relatives about japa? They may not know any names of God like the Indian mantras?

MM: They can repeat, "God, God" or "Divine".

Q: What can I tell people who are not interested in meditation, and do not yet know anything about spirituality?

MM: Tell them to do japa. You can talk about your own experiences. If they want they can also come for my Darshan.

Q: Mother, I feel that after nine years of meditation, I am craving something more. Because of this craving, meditation isn't what it once used to be. Do I have to be so rigid in the practice of meditation?

MM: If you don't feel like meditating, then it is better to do japa and also pray to God or the Divine. Feeling is more important than rigid practice. Flexibility is always helpful to grow further.

Q: I have two children aged ten and twelve years. Should they learn a technique of meditation?

MM: It is not necessary for children to meditate.

Q: I am always in a hurry to do things and I do not like to meditate. Then I think that it is stress, so I go for a horse ride. I relax. It is my way of meditation.

MM: When you ride on a horse, it is pleasure and it stays only for that time. But meditation is different. You have joy during meditation and after meditation.

Q: Is TM in conflict with the Mother?

MM: There are no conflicts with any techniques or sects or religions but you must be sincere to your own faith.

Q: I experienced the Supramental Light and lost unwanted body weight and my body was transformed. Did the Supramental Light cause this change?

MM: When you cannot sit quietly for ten minutes, looking here and there moving your arms and legs, your thoughts wandering somewhere, how can your body open to the Supramental Light? It is not possible.

Q: What shall I do to go to the higher worlds? Shall I eat less or shall I meditate more or worship or do japa more?

MM: It is not good to do one more or another less. To have balance in every action is good.

Q: In my daily life, I make many mistakes. How could I avoid them?

MM: Before starting any work, pray to God sincerely and offer your work to God.

Q: You have said that human beings are one, but their qualities are different. Could you kindly explain them?

MM: People have different qualities. Some people are emotional and given to outbursts. After they have released the emotion, they ask for forgiveness and so come to a compromise with themselves and others.

Some are selfish and they maintain selfish motives. These people believe in God only if they benefit from it. If they do not have any benefit, they turn against God. Even if they believe, they believe with a selfish motive.

Some people stay on a spiritual path as long as they have faith. Afterwards they leave.

Some people stay on the path no matter if they benefit or not. They focus on their goal, God, and continue to stay. Even if problems arise, they maintain faith because of their focus.

Some are only interested in knowing about worldly things.

There are some who are always waiting to find a mistake. If they find a mistake, they create conflicts. But there are some who show compassion even if they find a mistake.

Q: My aim is to change the film field to have higher values rather than current values because it will help change human nature, at least for a little while.

MM: Nowadays, the media has great influence on human beings. When people have time, they watch television or cinemas or films. If the cinemas are good, then it has a positive effect on human beings and if the films are violent it has a bad or negative effect. So it is better to have higher values.

Sometimes we cannot see the immediate effect on people when they see good films. But when the same people are in difficulties or in suffering or in depression, then the film comes like a flash into the mind and this will help them to think of God. To have higher values is a good and right attitude. These types of films do not bring money but they have a strong influence on the people. Other types of violent films bring money but they destroy human values.

Q: Childlike I am asking you, please give me strength to fulfil my deepest wish to make worthy films.

MM: Before starting your work pray to the Divine to give strength and also after finishing the work offer it to the Divine. I will help you.

Q: I feel I have obstacles to overcome to fulfil this ideal.

MM: Then pray to God wholeheartedly to remove all obstacles.

Q: Mother, could you kindly suggest to whom I can pray to remove the obstacles?

MM: Pray to the God whom you worship and ask God to remove the obstacles.

Q: Is a person special because of himself or because of his position in society?

MM: Man is not special. Because of his position in society, a man may have importance. Some are born with special qualities, some with a position and some with their profession. Some are born in a remote place and have name and fame in that place. But some are born in a remote place and have name and fame in another place. Then there are others who are born in a well known family and become famous through the family. But none of these positions in society or fame are important. Devotion to God is the most important.

అమ్మ

SPIRITUAL LIFE

Q: How do I lead a spiritual life in this world?

MM: Remember the Divine. Take care of your family and do your job. Try to do everything wholeheartedly and the Divine Grace will shower on you naturally.

Q: Is there a difference between the soul and the spirit?

MM: Yes. The spirit is part of the soul.

Q: What is the soul?

MM: The soul exists in every living being, wherever there is birth, growth and death. For example, every human being has a soul. In a human being the soul has the qualities of truth, peace, justice, self-giving, sacrifice, non-violence or harmlessness, right, duty, compassion, patience, wisdom etc. The soul has its own rules and principles. It guides us to be free from anger, falsehood, lust, greed, and violence. If we listen to it, then we have a happy and harmonious life. There will be no more suffering.

Q: Is one to forgive others?

MM: Forgiveness is a sign of spiritual progress. If you forgive others, God will forgive you.

Q: What do you think of friendliness?

MM: Friendship is one of the characteristics of bhakti.

Q: My greatest drawback is my anger. Could you kindly help me?

MM: Ego, stubbornness and anger are big enemies. Withdraw from these and you have ananda.

Q: I want to give money to the Mother but I have a family to look after.

MM: First take care of your family and later the Divine.

Q: In the world all my energies are drained and I am filled up when I come to Darshan. After some time when I go back I am empty again.

MM: Sometimes one must sacrifice oneself. If one has strong aspiration, then one will be filled again.

Q: Is giving up and surrender the same?

MM: When you give up something, usually you are expecting something, but surrender is without any expectation.

Q: It is very difficult to surrender completely.

MM: Try to surrender little by little.

Q: In my childhood I suffered a lot and my parents treat me very badly. In this situation, what can I do?

MM: Your parents gave birth to you. According to their knowledge, they taught you and they brought you up. Instead of fighting and quarrelling, it is better to be forgiving, grateful and love them. Then your sadhana will progress.

Q: What is your opinion on a giving nature?

MM: A giving nature plays a dynamic role both in daily life and in the spiritual life. Some people enjoy themselves by giving and other people will enjoy taking. A giving nature is a great gift on the path.

Q: Why is it great?

MM: When you give something which you love most and you offer it to God or to your master or to your family, then you have detachment from material life and at the same time, your love and devotion are growing towards God.

Q: I want to join the Mother Divine group for one year and then work in the outer world. I can meditate daily two hours there.

MM: I never encourage people to join in any groups or any techniques. You work in the world and when you have time then you can meditate in your home.

Q: What are the means we can use to reinforce our etheric body in order to have a strong physical body to help us face the many difficulties of life?

MM: A strong body is not necessary to face difficulties. Devotion, sincerity and prayer are essential.

Q: Are people who come to you really devoted to you?

MM: Because of their need or necessity they come.

Q: We are in a circle, i.e. we have our own ideas, feelings, love and experiences. We are in a limited circle. Is it possible to find the Divine with this limitation?

MM: When you come out of this limitation, then it is possible to find the Divine.

Q: What are the most important qualities to develop and what are the main defects to be destroyed in us?

MM: The correct attitude is to try to remember the Divine and to pray and ask for help to become conscious and to remove the defects.

Q: Is it necessary to ask only for spirituality?

MM: You can ask for everything.

Q: How do I offer my bad thoughts and feelings?

MM: Pray and ask God to take away the bad thoughts and feelings and ask for good thoughts and feelings.

Q: Why do human beings have egos?

MM: Do you believe that nowadays gurus have no ego?

Q: What is Light?

MM: We cannot understand the Light with the mind.

Q: What is surrender?

MM: Surrender is not weakness. It is a powerful weapon, the offering of yourself and the material world with which you have attachment.

Q: I am a bad person and I am afraid that you will see everything bad I have done.

MM: Do not be afraid. You are thinking that you are bad, not I.

Q: Is it possible for a human being to be always in the state of bliss?

MM: Even realised persons cannot always be in the state of bliss. As long as the body and the mind exist, it is not possible to be always in the state of bliss.

Q: Will Mother help to awaken the kundalini?

MM: Yes. But slowly.

Q: Is it good to do TM, Kriya yoga, Reiki and so on?

MM: All are different techniques. If you want to do them you can and also try to remember God.

Q: I spent a lot of money to learn techniques. Still I do not feel good or have any results. So I wish to ask for my money back.

MM: You gave money and for some time you enjoyed it. Now to ask for the money back is not fair. We do not buy the Divine through money.

Q: Many spiritual organisations take so much money to teach meditation? Is it necessary?

MM: No.

Q: I am twenty years old. I have no interest in continuing my studies. I want to meditate and lead a spiritual life.

MM: Life consists of different stages. In each stage, we have to follow the different activities. For example, at this age, you have to study. Afterwards you have to work, you may later marry and then have children. When your children are grown up and when you finish your responsibilities, then you spend most of your time in meditation or japa. But now it is better for you to continue your studies and when you have time, try to remember the Divine and do japa.

Q: I do not know how to offer the faults, mistakes or flaws in me to the Divine.

MM: How do you know that it is bad. Do not judge if it is good or bad. Just offer without judgement.

Q: When a woman serves a monk, is it true that she cannot realise the Divine?

MM: No. Whether it is a man or woman, when they serve with sincerity, they will certainly be enlightened.

Q: I want to realise the Divine today.

MM: If you don't do your duties, if you do not have a giving or serving nature or compassion or kindness for others, then you will never reach the Divine.

Q: What are the duties?

MM: Serve your parents. If you are married, take care of your wife and your children. If you do not fulfil these duties and want to realise the Divine, it is not possible.

Q: Which kind of suffering is most painful?

MM: When we desire and expect something, if we don't get it, that is most painful.

Q: How am I to be happy?

MM: Try to be content with what you have. You said that you tried to achieve something more but you did not get it and you are unhappy about the whole situation. Trying is good. But be happy whether you get it or not.

Q: What is the cause of unhappiness?

MM: All unhappiness is due to ego.

Q: That means, ego is the strongest of all?

MM: No. Necessity is stronger than ego.

Q: Is it true that when one is content, then it is the end of sadhana?

MM: Yes, contentment is one sign.

Q: I want to go on a pilgrimage to get peace. Should I go?

MM: Peace must be within yourself. You cannot get it from outside.

Q: What is patience?

MM: To accept all suffering without any sorrow. It is a sign of spiritual growth and also shows your sincerity and faith in the Divine.

> (Adilakshmi:) One day a man came to the Mother. He was very angry and restless. The Mother advised him to meditate. The man said:

Q: At the moment I have no faith in you or God or any religion.

MM: Meditation is to get rid of your anger and your restlessness. It has nothing to do with belief in God or religion. I am telling you to meditate to help calm your anger and restlessness.

Q: I have been doing yoga for a long time. Sometimes I feel good but sometimes it is unfulfilling.

MM: It is natural. Nature itself is not the same, all the time it is different. Sometimes it seems that life is blooming, harmonious and joyful. Life feels splendid like spring. There are some moments full of darkness, when anger, jealousy and all negative thoughts come out. It feels as though you are falling down, as if having slipped in the snow. These moments are normal. Offer them to God.

Q: What is the relationship between faith and doubt?

MM: Faith and doubt are part of human nature. You cannot escape from doubt or faith. Faith is the positive and doubt is the negative side of life. The person who has doubts suffers and it leads to destruction. If you have doubts, you close yourself with resistance and pull away from friends and family members, yourself and God, too. Doubt brings much suffering. You can destroy yourself with doubt. So do not concentrate on it as it is fruitless. Doubt will come and go. Do not give so much importance to doubt, otherwise it will grow bigger and bigger. Do not look into your doubting, just let it come and go. Pray instead for your faith to grow and do japa. If you focus on doubt it will grow bigger and bigger and if you focus on the faith it will grow. The aspect we focus on grows, either doubt or faith. The Divine will take care of us. Just have that faith, the Divine will help us.

Q: What gives satisfaction?

MM: There are different types of satisfaction or contentment. If you work hard with justice, then you have the contentment of your earnings. When you earn money based on your good deeds and morality and spend the money on good deeds, then you are cheerful and joyful with your action. With good thoughts, feelings, words and actions, you have the satisfaction of truthfulness. When one does one's duty wholeheartedly and sincerely, this gives the duty satisfaction. These are all signs of spiritual growth.

Q: Mother, I have a house, a car, a good job, enough money to pay my bills. But I am not satisfied with it and I want to make my family happier. So I want to have more money, at least a million rupees in my account for my future. So I want to start an import and export business and invest in the stock market. Please advise me.

MM: It is better to be content with what God has given you. Happiness does not depend on the money or outside circumstances but on the peace within you. Try to find peace and I will help you.

(Adilakshmi:) He did not listen to the Mother's advice and lost his money in the business and was in serious trouble.

Q: What is bad?

MM: To hurt others' feelings.

Q: Before I had no fear of existence but now I have fear. What is the cause of it?

MM: As long as we have faith in the Divine, there is no fear but when we lose faith, fear comes up.

Q: How to overcome it?

MM: Pray to God to remove the fear.

(Adilakshmi:) Mother's ways and actions are simple but with profound wisdom.

In the beginning the courtyard of our house was very rough with stones. In 1994, the Mother designed the pattern of the tiles for the courtyard. The workers came and did the design which the Mother desired. While they were working, the Mother helped them by adjusting the tiles or helping with other work. They felt at home with the Mother. Once they made a mistake by placing a wrong colour tile, instead of red they used black. It was almost done. Just then, the Mother came out of the house and saw the mistake from the balcony. Mother pointed out the wrong colour of the tiles which distorted the design. They were surprised about the Mother's precision and accuracy.

An American came for the first time and was surprised to see the courtyard. He asked me, "Who is the designer?. "The Mother", I told him. He said, "By birth I am a New Zealander. I settled in America. In New Zealand, some people painted on the walls of their houses the same design symbolising the steps leading to heaven. Isn't it true that the Mother is leading us to God!" I told the Mother about his comment on the design. The Mother listened silently.

The people in Thalheim have great appreciation for the courtyard and say that it is the most beautiful courtyard in Thalheim and add that Mother has brought good fortune to Thalheim and made Thalheim beautiful with Her presence. Now Thalheim is well known throughout the world. They are very proud of the Mother.

The Mother did this design simply. Her simple acts have high, rich and profound meaning in life.

అమ్మ

HELP AND GRACE

Q: How does the Divine Grace intervene?

MM: The Divine grace intervenes and often alters a given situation but many times it is neither possible nor desirable to eliminate karma completely. Grace can modify some of its effects.

Q: I would like to promote you in my circle of friends.

MM: No publicity. If your friends in your circle are in need of help, if they have problems, then you can talk to them. They will get help. Their faith itself will increase.

Q: I am in great agony and sometimes I love you and sometimes not. Can you help me?

MM: No matter if you love me or not, if you need the help, I will help you. The help does not depend on any condition.

Q: We do not have rains in Spain. Could you kindly help us?

MM: Yes.

> (Adilakshmi:) They had plenty of rain afterwards.

Q: I am phoning you today because today I came from the hospital. I am at home and have severe pain. Today I saw Mother's photo in the newspaper and I feel she is Divine. After seeing Mother's photo, I am free from pain. It is a miracle that she did for me. I would like to come and visit the Mother.

MM: First take care of your health. Rest and become strong. Pray to God and do japa. It is not necessary to come for Darshan.

Q: Mother, my wife is pregnant and now she is bleeding. Will you please help her to keep her pregnancy because the doctors have said there is no hope.

MM: Do not worry. Keep on praying. I will help you.

(Adilakshmi:) They had a girl and they are very happy.

Generally on every Friday, Saturday, Sunday and Monday between 4 PM and 5 PM the Mother answers the questions through Her secretary by phone. It is deeply moving to see how the Mother helps. Sometimes, people receive her help immediately. People ask for the Mother's help not only for themselves, friends and relatives but for their pets, too. It is a blessing to know and feel the Mother's help and how people are freed from their suffering. Their gratitude to the Mother is expressed in many ways.

One lady phoned and said that she had never been to the Mother, through her friend she had heard about the Mother. She greatly needed Mother's help:

Q: I have two sick cats and they are suffering and I get no sleep. I am also not healthy. Could you kindly help us to sleep?

MM: I will help you.

(Adilakshmi:) The very next day she phoned and said that the three of them slept well after the phone call. She apologised for not asking about the charge for the Mother's help in her suffering state. She was ashamed of her ingratitude and asked for Mother's address in order to express her gratitude. I told her that the Mother charges nothing. She was surprised and said, "You need money for living. We must give and do something for Mother."

There came a call from a housewife, who likes gardening. She worried about having a lot of snails in her garden which she had no control over and she did not know what to do.

Q: I have never had so many snails in my garden as this year. It is very difficult to control them. They are destroying the plants. Mother, could you kindly help me?

MM: Take the advice of a gardener. Pray to God and do japa that you will be free from this trouble. I will also help you.

(Adilakshmi:) Later, she phoned and said that after the phone call, the next morning when she went and searched for the snails, most snails had already left the place. Although there were still a few, they did not bother her. and she said it had been a big nuisance and a big problem. Now she is grateful to the Mother.

Once I was going to the Samadhi of Mr. Reddy. A nine year old boy from Thalheim came to me and asked, "Are you Mother Meera?" "No," was my answer. He told me that he wanted to meet Mother Meera. "Why?" I asked him. He said: "When we have a problem we can ask Mother Meera to help and Mother will help. So, now I have a big problem and I need the Mother's help. Could you kindly ask the Mother to help me?" He followed me to the Samadhi and asked me if we could pray here like in a church to solve our problem. I told him, "Yes, try." I was coming home and he followed me. I asked, "What is the problem?" "Do you know my mother slapped me?" "Why?" "I slapped my younger brother." I convinced him that he had to love his brother and not fight with him.

He came back to the house and once again asked to meet the Mother. I told him that it is not possible. He requested me to tell Mother Meera that he needs her help so that his mother will love him and not slap him. I went upstairs and told the whole story. The Mother smilingly answered that the Mother will help him and his mother but he also needs to love his brother and she gave him some chocolates. I conveyed the Mother's answer and gave him the sweets. The boy was so happy.

Now and then I see him when I go to the post office. Once he came and told me that now the situation has completely changed and his mother loves him and his brother also loves him and he is happy. He asked me to inform Mother about his gratitude.

The Mother comforts people during their troubles, however large or small, and people have such relief after their phone calls. For example, many people are afraid of dentists. A woman from the USA called, narrating that she has no fear of anything except the dentist. For three years, she had been suffering from a tooth pain but had no courage to go to the dentist. Now the pain was terrible. Still she could not decide whether to go to the dentist. She asked Mother for help. Mother told her:

MM: Do not be afraid. Before going to him pray to God to give strength and courage and peace to face the problem, and do japa and I will help you.

(Adilakshmi:) After visiting the dentist, she called back saying that everything went so smoothly and well with the grace of the Mother. She was astonished. Now she has no fear for the dentist and she is so grateful to the Mother that words cannot express her gratitude.

The Mother gave advice to a man from Great Britain who was crying on the phone saying that the very next day, he was scheduled for a big operation in which five of this teeth had to be taken out.

He phoned after a successful operation thanking the Mother for helping him at the dentist.

Sometimes, the Mother makes us feel light even in painful and heavy situations. This gives us strength so that we can go through the painful situation with courage and peace.

Mother helps even with mundane problems. Mother helped an eleven year old child to be free from homesickness and even helped her sick goldfish. The Mother's love and compassion is as vast as the ocean. Her love is not only for the human beings but also for animals.

Q: I had a rather strange experience while I was in India. We parked our motorbike in the shade of the only palm tree in a small village in the south of Goa. An enormous green coconut fell from a great height and hit me on the back of the head. I wasn't unconscious, but mildly confused and very delirious. I felt that I definitely was going to die. At first I was scared. I prayed to you over and over again. I called for you. I remembered afterwards that I distinctly called for you and Adilakshmi. I felt you both were there. I had a thought that because the chances were so slim of this accident, this must be my destiny. I didn't worry any longer about dying. Suddenly I felt much better and recovered soon after. Is there something in particular that I should learn from this?

MM: This experience enriches your faith in God.

(Adilakshmi:) A beautiful young couple from England came and stayed at Mother's home. They were working in the Mother's new house. After work they came home, and I asked them, "How was the day today?" He said that a miracle had happened to him. "I was climbing downstairs carrying a heavy load. There were no rails for the staircase. I lost my balance and was going to fall down the stairs. I would have been seriously injured. But somehow I stayed where I was and stood straight up without any motion. At that very moment, I was surprised to see the Mother at the bottom of the staircase looking at me. There are no words to express my gratitude to the Mother."

Afterwards I asked the Mother:

Adilakshmi: Ma, is it true, that knowing the danger of his falling down, you were there to protect him.

MM: Yes.

(Adilakshmi:) One of the devotees comes regularly for Darshan from UN in Switzerland. One day I asked him, "How was the trip?" He told me that he had narrowly escaped a fatal car accident and said that it was the second time the Mother had saved him from death. He added that during these two accidents he saw the Mother in the midst of the accidents. His life had changed completely. He has a different outlook about his relationships and his attitudes towards the world. Now, there is harmony in his home. He feels inner peace and he is more compassionate. His twenty years of meditation and practices had resulted in very little progress. Now his thirst for the Divine, that had been unsatisfied for the last twenty years, is quenched. He is tasting the Divine love. He wished he could find some words to express his gratitude to Mother.

I related the whole story and asked the Mother:

Adilakshmi: Mother! Did you save him from the accident?

MM: Yes.

(Adilakshmi:) A fax came from France addressing the Mother as Divine Mother, Saviour and an incarnation of God and giving thanks for Mother's special protection of their child. They narrated the incident as follows.

"A tragic incident occurred at our home, fortunately with a happy ending, but it upset us very much."

"Our little daughter is two and a half years old. She was dedicated to you at her birth. One day, while I was parking our car, backing our car in our driveway, my daughter ran out of the house towards me and the car. I could not see her as a huge tree blocked the view. She fell under the car as I backed up and the car ran over her but miraculously none of the four wheels touched her and she was saved without any injuries."

"I have prayed and meditated on you regularly for over twenty years. Although this incident upset me very deeply, at the same time it also increased and strengthened my faith in you in my heart. May the Divine Mother be praised!"

A fax came from Canada informing us what happened during a van accident. The man had been a devotee since 1979. He explained his experience as follows:

"On Sunday morning I woke up and looked at the blue sky and felt really calm and happy. I could feel your Presence very strongly. For that day, my girlfriend and I had planned to go and visit a park with wild animals that we could observe and touch. On the way we realised that we were on a wrong road and must go back by another road. It was getting late, so I pushed a bit on the pedal. All of a sudden: Bang! Bang! The front wheel blew up. I was doing about 125 KPH. There were cars all around and they could see that I was in trouble so they gave me room to regain control of the van. I found out that the outer belt of the tire was missing and only the inner belt remained! I was able to run very slowly to the nearest garage and get everything fixed. To my great surprise my girlfriend told me, 'We should join our hands and thank God because He saved us from something terrible.' So we did it in public. I feel that this day was blessed because of the very strong feeling of Your Presence I had felt in the morning. I also remembered the first time I asked,

'Mother, please be with me always.' You said: 'Remember God, I will be with you.' There is no doubt that you saved me and I am fortunate to know you, dear Mother!"

Mother always emphasises that it is not necessary to believe in Her. People can have their own faith and must be sincere in their aspiration to their God or Guru and if they need help, the Mother will help them. She strengthens their faith.

A person from USA had never seen the Mother but heard about her through her friends. She was in trouble and had some problems with her son and said that she had no desire to live. She and her son have their own faith. One day she asked the Mother to help her son in his job and to protect him. The Mother's answer was "Yes".

Some days later she faxed telling us that she had spoken with her son, who had told her that as he was driving his truck, a car from the opposite direction drifted into his lane and headed straight towards him. His attention had been diverted from the road but something alerted him just in time and enabled him to pull out of harm's way. He said that he was so shaken afterwards that it took him hours to grow calm again. But the result is that he feels absolutely certain that "something" was looking after him. This gives him greater trust in unseen protective forces. This experience also made his life feel precious to him. He thanked God and the Mother! His new faith has helped him relax from the pressures of his job search which had seemed so overwhelming before.

His mother says that she will eternally be grateful for the shielding power of Mother's amazing love.

It is always delightful to hear how the Mother helps people in their difficulties. A letter came from England from a Holistic Education & Training Centre with greetings for the New Year. They wanted to tell us about what happened to them as a group when they travelled to Thalheim last year. From the beginning of the journey until the end, the Mother protected the whole group. They wrote:

"Right from the start, I knew that we were being looked after. Just as we came off the highway, I felt we were running short of petrol. As I was sitting right at the back of the minibus, I did not know for sure, but something told me that there was a problem. I prayed to Mother Meera for Her help. We had only ten minutes left to catch the ferry, when my friend, who was driving, pulled off the highway and drove into a petrol station but it was closed. He turned back and drove into a different road and I saw a petrol station ahead of us. He slowed down and pulled into the station but stopped about three feet from the petrol pump. It was then I realised that we had run out of petrol just at that very moment. Some of us got out of the bus and pushed it the last few feet."

"None except myself had been to Mother Meera. We all had a wonderful and very moving Darshan with the Mother."

"On our way back to England in the minibus, I suddenly realised that there was smoke coming from somewhere. I called out to my friend who was driving saying that the bus was on fire. We were in very heavy traffic but just at that moment a gap opened up in the traffic and he was able to pull the minibus onto a part of the road which was being repaired by workmen. There was a lot of smoke by now, but no one was worried, we were all calm – as if everyone had the same thought, 'we were being taken care of.' The tyre at the front of the minibus had been punctured, but instead of it collapsing which it would normally have done (and that would have caused the bus to go out of control into the rest of the traffic) somehow, the tyre had stayed intact and upright for long enough to allow us to stop safely. As soon as we stopped, the tyre collapsed as if to say, 'I have done what was asked of me, now my job is finished.' My friend said he had never seen anything like it and that for a tyre to stay intact as we were driving at 100 KPH he would have thought was impossible."

"When we arrived back in England, everyone immediately came to sit in the meditation room and we gave thanks to Mother Meera for Her guidance. There was such a wonderful feeling of peace and joy among us. This feeling has never gone away from those who made the journey."

After reading this letter, I asked the Mother:

Adilakshmi: Ma, why should this happen to them, when they visit you.

MM: There is no special reason but this experience strengthens their faith in God.

Q: I heard through my friend that you help people who are in need. Is it true?

MM: Yes.

Q: I am an ordinary woman, I mean a non-philosophical person, very practical, hardworking, and much occupied. I have no children. We have been married for six years. We both want to have children. What can I do?

MM: Did you consult the doctor?

Q: Yes. The doctor said that we both are normal.

MM: Try to conceive a baby. Also pray to God whom you believe in and repeat the name of God to have the children. I will help you.

(Adilakshmi:) We received a call one month later that she was pregnant and thankful to the Mother. Two years later we came to know that she had another son.

Sometimes people write asking for help by letters or fax, sometimes through phone or through the secretary but rarely do they ask the Mother directly. Whatever way it may be, they get the help. When we are sincere, when we pray deeply and wholeheartedly, then we also get the help. There is no need for any

Adilakshmi and Mother 1996

language to ask for the help of the Divine. When our feeling is strong for the need, the Divine helps the needy. Not only human beings ask for the help but also animals ask for the help of the Mother in their own way.

It was one of the hottest summers in Germany. People said that the day was the hottest in the past 100 years. Late in the afternoon Mother and I were sitting in the living room and talking about different subjects to clarify my doubts about spirituality and reality and how God helps the needy whether man or animal and how the Divine satisfies hungry animals and saves their lives. I asked the Mother, "I heard that God helps all creatures and listens to their prayers and helps them." The Mother was listening and suddenly looked through the window into the garden. I turned and looked towards that part of the garden. I was surprised to see a young man near the small brook which flows between the garden and the back yard of the house, The Mother asked me to ask the boy to leave because he came to catch the fish. The boy left when I asked him. I saw two fish in the brook. I was happy that they were saved. I looked at the Mother. She smiled. My question was answered without words.

Nowadays Mother is busy with the new Darshan Hall. So there is no one to take care of the garden and the grass was overgrown. The Mother asked me to find the owners of some horses and inform them that they could feed their horses in our garden. I tried in vain for several days. I informed the Mother. She said that I must keep trying.

On one of the Darshan days, before going to bed, the Mother went to close the windows. The Mother saw a pony coming near the entrance to our garden. The Mother called me from the balcony. I was surprised to see the young pony in the garden. Someone from downstairs asked whether we should let it stay. The Mother said "let it stay, it will leave tomorrow." The next morning, when I looked for the beautiful young pony, it was not there.

The following fax came from the United States:

"I am a lawyer in the United States. Many people throughout the world believe that the legal profession in the United States is permeated with cynicism, manipulation, distrust and worse. The Darshan of Mother Meera is, of course, the opposite of the foregoing characteristics of the legal profession. Mother's Darshan is permeated with love, light, trust, and healing. Before receiving Darshan from Mother, as a lawyer with over 20 years of experience, I had seen and experienced the above trademarks of the profession. At Darshan, I experienced a light, a love, a healing unlike any other experience of my life."

"In February, 1992, I travelled to Germany to receive Mother's Darshan, intending to stay for one weekend for four Darshans. I stayed for three weekends and received twelve. Mother's light is changing my life."

"After I returned to the US, within days my partner presented me with the case of a woman with no money, 11 children, abandoned by her husband and who had fractured her cervical bone when falling out of a wheelchair while being wheeled into a hospital emergency room. Although the woman wanted 'her day in court', the case had previously been dropped by another lawyer who had abandoned her a month before the trial was due to begin. The case was ill-prepared. The lack of preparation made the case a loser. Since it was a medical malpractice case and there were no experts willing to testify, the case, seemingly, was hopeless. Mother's light, however, infused the entire case. Indeed, but for Mother's Darshan, I probably would not have accepted the case."

"From the beginning of the case, Mother's light seemed to envelop everyone involved, even the opposing parties and opposing counsel. Daily, for over a month of trial, I observed Mother's light falling like the soft rain on me, my client, the witnesses, the judge, defence counsel, and even the courthouse. Although the unfortunate woman, by any objective standard didn't have a prayer of winning the case, Mother's love and light prevailed. The jury deliberated for only about 20 minutes after a month-long trial, which is very unusual in itself, and returned a verdict for the woman. I believe Mother intervened in this matter, for reasons known only to her. Certainly, the moneys received from the jury verdict enabled the poor woman to get back on her feet and support her 11 children. Indeed, justice was done in this case, notwithstanding the improbable results. I began to realise that Mother's love is so vast, so pervading, yet so soft and humble, most of us are not generally aware of the whys and wherefores of her divine work. Gradually, I came to realise during the trial and afterwards that our prayers throughout the trial not only brought Mother's blessed help to the plight of this poor woman, but that her light even helped our opponent in arriving at a true and just result."

"I have learned that a simple opening to Mother's divine light in Darshan results in a humbling, yet powerful receipt of her blessings. These blessings unerringly guide the soul to everything needed in this life and beyond. A simple prayer from our heart and soul to forever surrender to her light brings us closer and closer to our goal – the true goal of every seeking heart: joyful union with God. Thank you, Mother, for the daily realisations you bring to us on this path."

అమ్మ

KARMA AND PAST LIVES

Q: What is karma?

MM: What you sow you reap, what you give you get, what you have done, good or bad, you will get in this life or in another life. Birth itself is karma. After your birth, by your own actions you are accumulating more karma. According to your actions you get karma. If you do good actions, then you get good karma. If you do bad actions, you will get bad karma.

Q: When we are born, how much comes from our parents and from heredity and how much comes from karma and impressions from past lives?

MM: There is definitely a part of man's make-up which comes from heredity, from the parents and even grandparents etc., but the main factor is our individual karma from our past lives.

Q: I have progressed very little in this life. Has my progress stopped or does it continue?

MM: Progress is not stopped but it continues life after life.

Q: What about karma?

MM: Karma is not determined. With our own actions we create our own karma. In olden times, if people could not solve their problems, they said that it was their own karma and they could not escape from it. By saying that they satisfied themselves. But we know that if we work hard, it is possible for us to live happily. But because of our idleness, we do not like to work and we seek escape by saying that it is our karma.

Q: Is it true, Mother, that each one chooses his or her parents according to one's karma?

MM: No.

Q: Which parent carries the child's karma? Is it true that the mother carries it until the child is 7 and the father until the child is 14 and the child after 14 carries his own karma?

MM: Karma is karma. We cannot say that until 7 or 14 the parents carry the karma of the child. Each one has to carry his or her own karma.

Q: How do we lessen our karma?

MM: Do good work, help people and have devotion and surrender to the Supreme or God.

Q: Can we be free from our karma?

MM: Action and its result cannot be avoided, but when we offer all our actions to God or the Divine with devotion and detachment, wholeheartedly and sincerely, then the actions will be purified and the result is that we are free from our karma.

Q: After phoning the Mother I rode a bicycle and had a small injury. I narrowly avoided breaking my neck.

MM: In life there is some karma that you cannot escape completely. With the grace even though you have an accident, it is minor and you escape greater danger.

Q: What will happen to me after I die?

MM: It depends on what you aspire for in life. If you aspire for material things you will get them. If you aspire for the Divine you will get the Divine.

Q: What does it mean to get the Divine?

MM: It does not mean to become the Divine. It means to move towards the Divine, to move onwards on the path leading to the Divine.

Q: Does it mean to become closer to the Divine or to be near the Divine?

MM: There is no near or far in the Divine. It means we are on the path.

Q: Mother, I was told by a doctor of psychogenetics who examined me that my lower back pain is inherited from five generations before me. Is this possible?

MM: No. Your pain has to do only with your present physical problems. Nothing to do with karma.

Q: Can an unhappy incarnation follow a happy one?

MM: Why not?

Q: I would like to know my past and my future.

MM: Do not think about your past or your future. Instead pray to God to fulfil your goal or ideal.

Q: I was born a Christian but I have strong faith in Buddha and also I respect all religions. I think, in my past, I was in India, maybe a Buddhist.

MM: It is not important if you were born in India. You have studied many kinds of religions and you like the way of Buddhism. So you are following it.

Q: I think in the past I did some good karma, so in this life I have had the opportunity to see several holy people.

MM: Presently, people generally concentrate only on money without having higher values. In a past life you wanted to serve humanity and so you are continuing in this life to help them.

Q: Can I have the strength to realise my aim?

MM: All will go well. You pray to God for strength and offer your work to God and surrender to God like a child. As your aim is good, all will go well and I will help you.

Q: You see all Gods and Goddesses. Which God is good for me to pray to in order to remove the obstacles?

MM: Pray to your beloved God to remove all obstacles and also ask for strength to fulfil your aim.

అమ్మ

ASTROLOGY AND RITUALS

Q: Why do you not believe in astrology or palmistry? In India people believe that it is better to travel only during the full moon but not on Amavasya (the last day of the lunar month on which the moon is invisible) and also not on Tuesday? Why do you not believe in astrology?

MM: When we were born, we were not born by choosing a date. When we die, we do not die by choosing a date. In life, birth and death are important. Birth and death we cannot decide. Therefore, if we depend for other matters on astrology, it is mere foolishness. People say that we should not travel during Amavasya because it is dark. Anyone may come and attack you or someone may come and threaten to kill you or thieves may come to steal. It is dangerous to travel in the dark but the day itself is not a bad day. If we travel in the daylight, people will be there and light is there. There is less danger when we travel in the day. There is no higher meaning behind it.

Q: Is conducting yagnas good?

MM: I do not encourage yagnas, homas, or other rituals. I emphasise only japa which has neither rules nor regulations but when you say the name of God from the heart it has effective fruits. You cannot buy the yagna or homa. If you want to do yagna or homa you must be present there physically to conduct them. Then you will get the fruit of the yagna.

Q: Mother, we were instructed to donate large sums of money for yagnas. Is this necessary?

MM: When we want to perform homas or yagnas we must be present physically. If we are in one place and these are done in another place, then it is of no use to perform them.

Q: Have you ever done any puja or homa?

MM: Yes. In 1990 I did Bhumi Puja (worship of Goddess Earth) and Durga Homa in 1993.

Q: What was the purpose?

MM: People told me that if I paid money for Durga Homa, on my name they will do it, but the Brahmin or Pujari or priest told me that the person must be physically present to do Homa. So it was inevitable for me to be there and do it.

Q: Is using a pendulum helpful?

MM: No.

Q: Are certain kinds of healing practices good and others not?

MM: I never recommend any particular type of healing.

Q: I believe in angels. How can I feel their presence?

MM: It is true that angels exist. It depends on what you expect from them. If you ask for help, then you will get help.

Q: Mother, are pujas and homas necessary?

MM: To worship God is good. Doing puja with some expectation like getting enlightenment or expecting some fortune to come is not good.

Q: Mother, is Jyotish or astrology necessary for enlightenment?

MM: If you have money you will try many things. If you are a multimillionaire and you are sick, your sickness is treated differently than if you are poor. Jyotish has nothing to do with enlightenment.

Q: Mother, are gems necessary for the offset of negative karma?

MM: Because you have money, you will buy and keep them with you. If it is true then what about poor people. Gems cannot free us from negative karma.

Q: Mother, is it necessary to study the Vedas for enlightenment?

MM: By studying the Vedas or other holy books you get knowledge but not enlightenment. Many people studied the Vedas and also dedicated their life to learning the Vedas. Please go and ask them how many are enlightened.

Q: Someone advised me that my fortune is not good, so it is better to do homa, yagna and worship (puja) in the temple. Is it true?

MM: To do puja is good but expecting that if we do puja, we have good fortune, that attitude is wrong. The priests (pujaris) do pujas every day but they are not happy and they have no peace. Always there is one problem or another. They do puja with a restless mind and heart and if they cannot solve their own problems with their own prayers, how can they solve others' problems?

Q: An astrologer said that there is a possibility I may have a car accident. Is it true?

MM: Most people here in the West have cars and the astrologer told that you might have a car accident. But in India, the Indian astrologer says that they may have an accident by car or bicycle or bus or lorry. In India people walk on the road, so any of the above mentioned vehicles can cause an accident. It is common sense and it is nothing special that the astrologer foresees the accident. If the astrologer knows only western life, his interpretations are one way, if he knows only the east his interpretation is different. If he knows both east and west, his commentary is different again.

Q: I should like to learn pendulum? Is it good to learn it, Mother?

MM: It is not good to consult the pendulum. Two things are important. One is to believe in God and the other is to have self-confidence. If you practice the pendulum, then you will grow in the habit of consulting the pendulum for each small matter, and the pendulum gets more importance than your self-confidence and your belief in God.

అమ్మ

CHANNELING AND MESSAGES

Q: I received information from a person who claims to work under the guidance of Mother Meera and also claims to transmit Paramatman Light to others and charges money for doing so. Is this information true?

MM: I have never authorized anyone to represent me or to act on my behalf and I have never trained anyone to help me in my spiritual work. I have to do my work by myself. People project their own ideas onto me and they like very much to follow them.

Adilakshmi: Frequently, people say that Mother has told them, telepathically or in a dream, to come to Her or that She has given them instructions to do something. Mother does not work in this way. She wants people to deal with the issues and challenges of their lives directly and practically. No imagination, it is better to be realistic.

Q: Today, someone told me that Mother had called him to come and visit Her. Is this true?

MM: This is not true. I never call anyone to come to me. If people want to come to Darshan, they should telephone to make an appointment for a visit. I don't like people to come without appointment nor wander near the house.

Q: I received an inner message from Sai Baba in which he told me to go to India to be with him. Should I follow or believe in such messages when received in this way?

MM: This is only your imagination. You may visit him during your regular holidays. Don't quit your job for spiritual reasons. You can make spiritual progress when you work.

Q: Sometimes I hear your voice telling me to do this or that. Shall I follow the voice?

MM: Use your common sense. Do not give any particular importance to what you see in your visions or what you hear and what you experience.

Q: Is it helpful for me to consult a clairvoyant, channeler or healer for my personal development?

MM: If you believe in God it is not necessary to run here and there. If you are sincere you can achieve everything. You have to accept the responsibility for your life and you must take it into your own hands. Be strong and positive and try the best you can. Do not go through others or through anything else.

Q: What if I am sick?

MM: Go to a doctor immediately and pray to God. I will help you, too.

Q: My friends knew several clairvoyants, astrologers and healers. It was fascinating for me to learn what my friends heard about themselves. Is it good to consult such people?

MM: It is not necessary to go to all those people. Each would tell you a different solution for the same problem. They confuse people. They cannot see all and therefore it is confusing for you. It is more important to do japa and pray to God or the Divine.

Q: I saw in my dream that you were asking me to come and see you. Is it true?

MM: No. In reality, I am not asking you to come.

Q: But in the dream it was so clear that you asked me to come.

MM: You are talking about your dream state. Many times people say that I said this or that in a dream. I am telling you now that it is wrong but you do not believe me. After my departure people will say that Mother said this and Mother said that.

Q: In my dream I was told not to look for any new job but rely more on you.

MM: Continue your job and rely only on the Divine, do not give any importance to dreams.

అమ్మ

RELIGION

(Adilakshmi:) All religions are manmade to reach the Divine. All have the same goal but they are different paths. It is just like coming to Mother Meera. People who are near by come by walking, some come by bus or car or by train or by ship or by plane. Whatever may be the vehicle or direction to come to the Mother, everybody's aim is the Mother.

Q: Many religions are fighting with each other and killing in the name of their God. Are the religions in the world going to change as man evolves?

MM: No, as long as human beings have different religions, the fighting will continue. There will be no end.

Q: Only when man sees no difference in his religious faith and other religious faiths will the conflict end?

MM: Yes.

Q: When I am reborn or reincarnate, is it necessary to be born in the same religion?

MM: Religion is manmade. However it is not a bar. You can be born in any religion.

Q: First I believed in Jesus. After some time I lost faith in him. I saw your photo in my friend's house and I felt renewed faith. After many years with you I returned to my faith in Jesus but I still had faith in you. Now I have lost faith in you.

MM: It is a good thing that you returned to your faith in Jesus. That is important. It is not so important that you have lost faith in me. To regain faith in Jesus is important. Pray to Jesus and surrender to God.

Q: What do you think of Christianity?

MM: The greatness of Christianity is to help humanity.

Q: I am practising Buddhism and I want to pray to the Mother but I am afraid that I will not keep my promise of commitment to the rituals.

MM: When marrying, we also promise much but do not fulfil our promise.

Q: Adilakshmi, you told us that the Mother transcends all Vedas. How?

Adilakshmi: The Vedas were written by highly developed conscious human beings, Rishis or Sages. They teach us how to attain the Divine and what patterns and ways of life one must lead in daily life in order to achieve one's goal or to unite with the Divine. But Mother Meera is divine and Her each action, each word, is divine.

Q: Is it true that Mary appears in Colorado? Is it good to go and visit?

MM: It depends on your faith and belief. When we know that it is a holy place, it is good to visit.

Q: Is God only in temples, churches, and mosques?

MM: Even if there are no temples, no churches, and no mosques, the Divine Power is always there. These are manmade things.

అమ్మ

MARRIAGE AND FAMILY LIFE

Q: Is marriage an obstacle for the divine realisation?

MM: Marriage is not an obstacle for divine service or for reaching the Divine. Do not struggle to take the decision whether to marry or not. If you want to marry, it is OK. If you want to remain a nun or a monk it is also OK. But do not strain yourself, make a free decision and live as you want, alone or with a companion.

Q: I am taking pills for birth control. Is it good?

MM: One must know oneself.

Q: Who needs more love?

MM: Children and old people need more love and care.

Q: Why do Indians give more importance to marriage than Westerners?

MM: If Indians had the same freedom and prosperity as Westerners then Indians also would not give marriage as much importance. In Indian culture, marriage is necessary or essential. Even a millionaire or an emperor would like to give his children in good marriages with prosperous futures. When all of his children are happy then he thinks that he has fulfilled his Grihasta Dharma (the duty of the family).

Q: Is it necessary to have children?

MM: Yes. I think it is necessary to have children.

Q: Why?

MM: If I give you an explanation. then you think that I have an Indian mentality. To maintain the family is important. When you are sick or in trouble, then there is somebody to help and to look after you. Family support nourishes the human nature.

Q: If I am ill, I will go to the hospital. There a nurse will look after me. I do not need a family.

MM: Yes. It is true that the nurse will look after you. The nurses will fulfil their duties. But there is a difference of love and affection when given by the family, such as husband or wife, father or mother, son or daughter, brother or sister. Such family members serve you and nurse you on a very subtle feeling level which nourishes you.

Q: Recently I saw in my friend's family that one of the children was praying that his father would die due to his disease but the other children on the contrary were praying that he would recover from the disease.

MM: Yes. I know that but we have to accept both good and bad.

Q: I have inner mental pain. What can I do?

MM: In your case, there is no inner mental pain. There are only outer problems. When you see clearly the outer problems, then you will not feel the pain. Try to solve the problems, then you will be free from the pain.

Q: Should children of all cultures be required to study the Vedas?

MM: At present, if we educate a child to study the Vedas, when he wants to get a job, then it is difficult to find a job, and life will be difficult. In the past, in India, it was appropriate to study the Vedas according to that time and culture. But at the present time even in India it does not help people to solve their problems. We must provide the education according to the present time, so that in the future the children will not suffer because of our choices.

Q: I am a householder and the mother of five children. So I am always busy with my household work. I want to devote more time to God but cannot. I am unhappy about it.

MM: Is there harmony and love in the family?

Q: Yes.

MM: Is it a successful family?

Q: Yes. They are all grown up and well established in their lives.

MM: It is a good sign for spiritual progress when you give up or devote yourself to others. This brings to fulfilment a sacrificing, giving nature which is a fundamental quality for spirituality. In giving you get happiness and satisfaction. It is the result or fruit of spirituality. Family life is very important. If everyone in the family is happy, then the world will be happy and we will have less problems.

Q: My husband is not spiritual. What can I do?

MM: You cannot judge if he is spiritual or not. He has his own way of spirituality. So let him be free in his own way. Is he in harmony with you?

Q: Yes. He does not meditate but makes things easy for me during my meditation schedule. He is co-operative. He also listens carefully when I narrate my experience.

MM: When he is harmonious and understanding with you that itself is a sign of spirituality. So let him be in his own way. But you can pray and do japa for him.

Q: I love my husband and he also loves me. Sometimes we fight and he hits and hurts me. It is impossible for me to bear this pain. So I want to separate from him.

MM: If both have love, then it is better to live together. Sometimes it is better, if one is calm minded, to have fewer outbursts of anger. When people live together, sometimes when one is angry it is better for the other to be silent.

Q: We had been married for 15 years and then he left me. I have no hope that he will come back. What can I do?

MM: When you have no hope, then try to find another man who is single, and continue to live your own life.

Q: Does one need to be like a child?

MM: Yes, but in the present time children are more mature than in the past.

Q: I would like to have a life partner who is beautiful, rich and spiritual with all the good qualities and I have waited for a long time. What shall I do?

MM: To have a partner according to your imagination will not happen. We have to adjust ourselves to what life brings.

Q: How can I know when I meet someone that she is the right person?

MM: The love itself shows and also you feel it.

Q: I am depressed. How long do I have to wait for a life partner?

MM: When we want some specific qualities in a life partner, it is not easy to find one according to our taste or liking. We have to wait and have patience and pray to the Divine or God and also do japa for our wish to be fulfilled.

Q: I am Indian. My son wants to go to USA for higher education. Should I send him?

MM: If you have the possibility to send him to USA, you can send him but you should not take more dowry because of that if he returns to India. (In Indian tradition, the father of the bride has to give property or money to the husband.)

Q: We thought that my father had died but we were surprised to see him at my grandmother's funeral. We are all angry because he did not take care of us. My mother also died when I was ten. How should I behave with my father?

MM: Past is past. So now your father is with you. Do not fight with him but love him.

Q: Suriyoga people are going to hold a meeting for peace in Russia. I am one of the members of the group. I cannot decide if I should go or not because then I have to leave my child. I am unhappy to leave the child and he too is unhappy. There is a group of 150 ladies that will go there and pray for peace.

MM: If you have no peace, how can you give peace. First make your family happy and peaceful. First you must have peace.

Q: I am a student and I want to help mankind. Which direction shall I go?

MM: What do your parents advise?

Q: My father asked me to take care of a business but I do not like it. I want to help others.

MM: If you do not help your father, how can you help others? First make your family happy and do what your father asked you to do.

Q: Some say that each abortion means to kill Jesus. Is it true?

MM: If it is true, then all who are born and grown up human beings must be Jesus.

Q: I have a friend and we have now become lovers. Sometimes he is a terror. What can I do?

MM: There are two possibilities for you: to accept the situation as it is or try to find a new friend.

Q: Who is a real friend?

MM: A real friend helps you when you are in need and protects you and your prosperity. When you are horrified or frightened, he gives you shelter. He will be with you in your prosperity and in poverty. He tells you his secrets and keeps yours, too. He is with you in your difficulties. He sacrifices his life for you. He also gives you the proper advice and is compassionate in your difficulties. He is happy for your prosperity, name and fame. He cannot tolerate someone disgracing you. He advises you to do good and leads you on the right path. He discourages or warns you against doing evil. It is difficult to find a real friend.

Q: Why does the Western family break down but not the Indian family?

MM: First, in the West when there is no satisfaction in the sexual relationship, then both will look for another relationship. The man will secretly go to another woman and the wife will secretly go to another man. When each one comes to know about the other relationship, both will suffer and then struggle to come to a compromise, trying to mend the relationship and at the end when it is not possible then they separate.

Secondly, when they have children, there is a difference in their sexual relationship and they look for a new relationship.

In India, we do not have financial and sexual freedom and also the marriage is arranged by the parents or elders or other family members. Even though some people have all kinds of freedom, still they are afraid to choose their partner because of their culture and also their religious background. They are afraid of karma, of doing something wrong, thinking that the Divine is in everything and they offer their desires to the Divine.

Even in India there are some cases where people are free, but they are not respected in society. In some cases they are not allowed in the temples and in social gatherings, marriages or festival gatherings.

In western countries because of sexual freedom, people tend to live together for only some time. When their sexual life is not fulfilled, they separate. At that moment, they do not see or realise that they are breaking up their own families and also other families. When they fall in love on an emotional level only, they do not comprehend how much they are damaging each other.

When people concentrate only on the fulfilment of their sexual desire, nothing else, then husband and wife deceive each other. Even if husband and wife both live together in the same house, the husband has a physical relationship with another woman and the wife has a physical relationship with another man. They neglect their children.

Q: How did so great a difference develop between Indian families and western families?

MM: Indians believe in reincarnation and they also believe in karma but westerners generally do not believe in these principles.

Q: Why do western children often hate their parents?

MM: The children hate their parents because when the children need the father, he is not there and when they need the mother, the mother is not there to fulfil their needs. When the children mature, naturally they hate their parents.

Q: How can parents avoid the hatred of their children towards them?

MM: The father or the mother should be a good example for their children. Children have very tender and delicate hearts and minds. At this age, we should not hurt their feelings because this has such strong imprints or impressions on them. These are never erased from their hearts and minds. It is better not to cause children to suffer. If possible try to give them happiness and peace. The impressions of childhood, good or bad, have great impact on them. As you gave birth to the children, it is your duty to take care of them and also to fulfil their needs. Until twelve years, the children need the most help. Until sixteen years, the parents should continue to take care of their children. If they don't need your help and assistance, then it is different. Generally, the future of the children depends on the parents. If the child is good or bad mostly depends on the parents.

Q: In the West, what is the best way to solve problems in the relationship of husband and wife?

MM: If there is no harmony between husband and wife, it is better to separate. If you seek a new partner, then it is better to find a single person. One should not destroy the family life of another to satisfy one's sexual desire, one should not interfere in their family life and break their relationship. If you help them, then the Divine will also help you. There are generally minor differences in the husband-wife relationship. One should not use those differences to interfere in order to gain physical intimacy. Sexual relationship should not be used to console the problems in others´ marriage. Generally do not involve yourself in the marriage of others. Solve the problems in your own marriage, or separate. It is very bad to cause separation in another marriage. In marriage, the sexual desire must be balanced. Generally there is no end to sexual desire. The more you desire, the deeper the trap. It is fathomless. In marriage, it is better to concentrate on the needs of the children, not your own. It is better to build strong values and character in the children by faithful adherence to your duties. When sexual desire replaces the duties of a mother or father, children suffer deeply. The minds and hearts of the children are damaged and psychological problems result. Try to bring harmony into your family by faithful devotion to God and your duties. If possible, you may pray for the family of another, but do not interfere in the marriage of another.

You should think about and remember the past of your society, how it was 10, 20, 30, 40, 50 years ago and how your society is now. Compare it yourself. There is nothing that I need to tell you about it. Try to bring harmony into your family. If possible, you can also pray for the families of others.

Q: We are unhappy. We have parents but we feel we do not have them. We are six children. I am 18 years old and my youngest brother is only two years old. My mother is only interested in her romantic life and she has no interest in taking care of her children. My father is OK when compared to my brothers' and sisters' fathers. When we come back from school there is no one to look after us. We have to take care of ourselves. There is no happiness or joy in the house. Sometimes there is unbearable sadness among us especially during Christmas. One of our fathers comes and the others feel terribly unhappy. The joy of Christmas has melted away. What shall we do to gain harmony, peace and joy? Is there any solution, Mother?

MM: In this case your mother must herself realise her mistake in what she is doing and she must come out of it by herself. All of you must pray for her and I will help you.

Q: Is it God's Will that I must be alone?

MM: It is not God's Will. If you want to lead a family life and want a partner, then try for it and pray for it and do japa.

Q: Are children in Europe different from children in India?

MM: Yes.

Q: In which way?

MM: Here parents do not give enough love. Children feel the lack of love.

Q: Here the children are suffering more. What do you think, Ma?

MM: Here in the West people do not get love. The children are free and the parents fight in front of the children and do everything in front of the children. But in India, the parents have privacy and the children are not as free as here.

Q: I am in love and I have a problem because it is one-sided.

MM: If both have love for each other, then there is no problem. If it is one-sided. then the problem becomes bigger and bigger.

Q: Is it good for children to live in the ashram and go to school?

MM: It is better for the children to stay with the parents and they can go to any school. If they stay with the parents, then love blossoms and they have a good relationship with the parents.

Q: Is it true that if the mother or the father of the family is efficient and devoted to the dharma, the whole family will have the blessings of the Divine?

MM: Yes.

Q: How?

MM: When parents are sincere and hardworking, the children follow the footsteps of their parents and the parents are good living examples and models for the children.

Q: When should I retire from my family duties?

MM: If you have children, then it is your duty to educate them, to find a job for them and arrange marriage and make them self-sufficient. When your children have children, then it is their duty to look after their children. If you take the responsibility also for your grandchildren, then it is ignorance. In the West, the same duties apply without arranging marriage.

Q: I have been living in America for more than 40 years, during which time I have served as a doctor. Now I want to live in an ashram but my wife wants to live independently without an ashram because ashram life requires an offering. We have great conflict. What shall I do?

MM: Live independently and visit different ashrams and donate what you want and serve as much as you can.

Q: How should one approach family relations?

MM: One should feel each relationship as it is. Don't mix them. For example, see your mother as a mother, sister as a sister, brother as a brother and father as a father. Do not approach one another with sexual intentions, because then many problems arise. There is no harmony and peace in the family and troubles start. Nowadays people are mixing these relations. These are human beings, just evolved from animal to man and there is not enough soul development. Sin is piled up like a mountain, and goddess Earth (Bhumata) cannot tolerate the sins of human beings. It is the result of the sins and actions of human beings that now there are so many catastrophes and so much destruction in the world.

Q: What is the main thing to avoid or to develop or to cultivate?

MM: There is nothing in particular to avoid or to cultivate. Just try to lead a normal good life, do japa and aspire for the Divine.

Q: When we feel the love of the Mother, one finds that Love exists at this crucial time and then it seems that Love goes away.

MM: Love always exists. Only sometimes when we are closed, then we do not feel it but when we are open then we feel that Love exists.

Q: Before I met you I hated my parents and did not have harmony with my mother and father. But after meeting You I find harmony and love for my parents. Is it true that I really love them? It is difficult for me to understand.

MM: Yes. It is true. You do not need to doubt it.

Q: Please help me to understand other people and how to live in harmony with them.

MM: When your consciousness grows it is easy to understand.

Q: Why do people fight and why are there wars?

MM: There is no love and no friendship. So the result is war.

Q: In my daily life, I make many mistakes. How should I avoid them?

MM: Before starting any work, pray to God sincerely for perfection and offer your work to God.

అమ్మ

HEALTH AND MEDICINE

Q: Is physical suffering necessary for evolution? Can intense work on oneself make us heal completely?

MM: Not necessarily.

Q: My wife has breast cancer and she is suffering so much and is depressed. We have never come for Darshan. Mother Meera, please help my wife.

MM: It is not necessary to be depressed. Have confidence in God and pray to God to help her. Relax and try to be peaceful and I will help.

Q: My father is suffering from cancer and the doctors doubt that the medications which they are giving are working. Is it better to stop it or is it the wrong medication?

MM: It is the right medication. Only the illness is serious. Even though the medication has no effects, it gives satisfaction to the patient. So it is necessary.

Q: My wife has chronic headaches and no doctor can find out the cause.

MM: Drink more water and do regular exercise.

Q: I feel guilty that due to me my friend has got arthritis. What can I do?

MM: If he has mental shock or a nervous breakdown, then you may think that maybe you are the cause of it. For a physical disorder like rheumatism for example, it is purely physical. It is not because of you.

Q: People who are suffering from AIDS are afraid of God. Is it because of their sins they have this disease?

MM: Being afraid of God is not helpful. They should pray to God for help. If you are feeling guilty about your actions, then you can ask for forgiveness for what you have done.

Q: I am sick and believe that the doctors cannot help me.

MM: First let go of the idea that you are sick. Don't give importance to your being sick and do not run away. Try to do all the activities you generally do. Do not let others influence you to believe you are sick. Sometimes people around us make the problem worse in order to gain something or they are jealous or by showing sympathy they want to dominate. So be vigilant and aware of the situation. Surrender to the Divine, offer your sickness to the Divine and also ask for strength to release the idea that you are sick. I will help you.

Q: I am sick. When will I be normal again?

MM: It is better to think that you are normal and healthy. Lead a normal daily life and work. When you come out of the idea that you are sick, then you will become normal. Have a strong will power and pray to God for it. I will help you.

Q: I had an eye operation. But I lost my sight completely. Now, I live in fear and worry.

MM: Do not worry. By worrying, you will lose your peace of mind and happiness and still will not get your sight back. Instead, pray to the Divine, grow in the confidence of the Divine, have faith in the Divine and turn your thoughts towards the Divine, and pray to the Divine to help you. You will discover inner vision.

Q: Nursing and health-care generally in Europe has been strongly influenced historically by Christian tradition and lately by humanistic perspectives. Some people suggest that unless a nursing practice subscribes purely to orthodox Christian principles, then we should have nothing to do with it. Indeed, some would say it is the work of the devil if it is not seen as purely Christian. What are your views on this?

MM: The motive of Christianity to help others is a great and good work. The aim is good.

Q: Many nurses and other health-care workers, especially those in the restructuring former communist countries of Eastern and Central Europe, have historically found it difficult, if not impossible, to marry a spiritual perspective with their day to day work, not least because of a political system in which they lived which forbade any mention of the notion of a divine will at work. Now as the old system falls apart many nurses find themselves unclear about their purpose or direction and are searching once again for meaning and purpose in their work. What advice can you offer them?

MM: Each individual believes in the existence of a higher Power consciously or unconsciously. So, people can pray deep inside and it is not necessary that the others know what they do.

Q: In the West as well, in recent years, nurses have found themselves increasingly divorced from any thought of the spiritual basis of their practice. Florence Nightingale, a well known British nurse who, it is largely accepted, laid the foundations for modern nursing, based much of her work on Christian principles. Many feel that recent decades have seen this being lost from nursing. For example, many nurses are taught to see human beings as little more than biological machines with diseases which require treatment. When patients have religious needs, nurses are given little encouragement to address them, rather to hand them over to a particular minister of religion. It has become very difficult for nurses to even mention the word God in their practice or to understand how spiritual principles, as opposed to humanistic ones, may guide them. What would be your response to this?

MM: When the patients themselves have no faith in God, what can the nurses, priests, or doctors do?

Q: Enormous numbers of nurses suffer from high levels of stress in their work. Many have stress related illnesses and have long periods of sickness or absence from work and high rates of mental health problems and suicide. Do you think that following a spiritual path can help nurses with problems like these and if so, how?

MM: Naturally the above problems arise because the people have less faith in God. When you have full confidence in God, then the problems will become less.

Q: Do people have to come to you personally to receive help and if not, how may we seek your guidance?

MM: It is not necessary to come to me. People should stay where they are and pray to God, or have their own faith and do japa, that is, to repeat the name of God sincerely and wholeheartedly and ask for what they need. I will help and guide them.

Q: Nurses deal on a day to day basis with an enormous range of human suffering and tragedy. What advice can you give that would help us deal with the suffering of others?

MM: They can pray to God and ask God for help to remove the suffering and pain of the patients.

Q: What can we do to ensure that we ourselves do not become dragged down and harmed by witnessing the suffering of others?

MM: Nurses give service to the patients. It is of no use to identify with their sufferings. Instead they can encourage the patients wholeheartedly and pray to God for the betterment of the health of the patients. If possible, they can console the patients with feelings. It is good to do so.

Q: Many people believe, Florence Nightingale once said, that nursing is the finest art, by which one human being can express the caring and compassion for another. Is this simply because some human beings are better able to offer care to their fellows than others or do you see it as a wider part of a Divine purpose?

MM: All cannot do the service. Some people will be upset by seeing others suffering and there are others who are upset just by hearing the name of a hospital, and want to be far from the hospital. Florence Nightingale's saying is true. They have that quality of service, so they can offer the service.

Q: In many countries, nurses are struggling with ethical dilemmas where they find it hard to know what is right or wrong. How can nurses seek guidance to help them with the difficult dilemmas they face in their day to day work?

MM: We cannot say this is good or that is bad or right or wrong. We have to act according to the circumstances and offer it to God, good or bad.

Q: Many nurses have become concerned at the increasing demands for euthanasia. Some people are asking that when they become old or frail or disabled they should be helped to end their lives. Others see it as a right to help end the life of someone who is suffering or in pain. Yet others see it as very expensive to care for all those who are sick or disabled and so it would be much cheaper if we helped them to die sooner. Nurses frequently have to work with the people who are directly affected by these issues. What should be our response?

MM: It is better and also good to depend on God, and do our duty. Whatever we do, good or bad, offer it to God and ask God for forgiveness. Whatever the mistakes we have made offer them to God. This is the only thing that will save and protect us.

Q: Why do you advise people to go to a doctor?

MM: Some people say that they are afraid of doctors, others say they have no confidence in doctors and some want to meditate to cure their disease. But this is not the way to cure a disease. Due to this, I suggest people go to a doctor.

Q: Beloved Mother, is it good or wrong to give away organs or parts of the body after death. I always thought the soul will leave the body after death. But one of my friends told me you cannot go on your path if still parts of your body are kept in other people. Could you kindly clarify this issue?

MM: Even if some parts of the body are taken out after death and placed in a living human being, still the soul has separated from the body. There is no relation between body and soul in these circumstances.

Q: Some are so sick that they can only live with the help of medical appliances. With the help of this apparatus they can live, without it they will die.

MM: In such cases the person should decide if he wants to continue to live with the help of the apparatus or die without it.

Q: I have a problem with my back. When I walk it is painful. The doctors advise different treatments. The medical doctors say they want to do surgery to find out the cause. The chiropractors say that with some adjustment the pain will stop. What advice shall I follow?

MM: If you have confidence in chiropractic, first you follow it. If it does not help, then you can follow the advice of medical doctors.

Q: What is the Mother's opinion about Ayurveda?

MM: It is mainly done with plants. In India it is a poor man's medicine. Here it is expensive and people who have money can afford to have it.

Q: Is it necessary to be proficient in pulse diagnosis?

MM: No.

అమ్మ

DEATH AND SUICIDE

Q: What is Death?

MM: Death and Life are God's creation. You cannot separate the two. In fact none is born and none dies.

Q: Is it true that when one surrenders to God, then one is pure at death?

MM: When one's surrender is perfect, then one will be pure even at death. At the time of death, one has no desire at all.

Q: What happens after death?

MM: People have so much attachment to their family, friends and material life. When the soul has attachment, it will be here for some time, and souls who have no attachment will leave this earth plane.

Q: Most religions say that suicide is wrong, it is a sin, or it creates bad karma in the next life. In certain cases the ending of life is tormented with terminal illness or grave pain and difficulty, such as AIDS or cancer. Many people all over the world are contracting AIDS, and so many AIDS sufferers in the world commit suicide. May I know your opinion?

MM: There are many reasons why people commit suicide. If there is not enough love or one is deceived by love, or a business partner deceived the other or there is failure in the business or when there is some loss, people become depressed. Sometimes it is simply the failure to fulfil a desire, and sometimes it is illness. To escape from problems, it is not good to commit suicide. We can solve them through prayer to God. We have to solve our problems when we are alive. We cannot solve them after our death.

Q: Some people die in accidents like plane crashes or other unexpected events. What happens to them?

MM: The people who die in accidents do not know that they are going to die in such a way. But God or Paramatman knows the fate of these persons, that they are going to die in this way. So He takes them in His glorious Light. Only God will look after them, but we can pray for them and also ask God to help them. God is the only saviour.

Q: In a book published in 1915 written automatically through a spirit (a person who had died in 1913) there is a description of a World War I battlefield where the souls of soldiers killed in battle were confused and didn't know what to do after death.

Thalheim, Germany 1994

MM: People have little faith in the Divine. When they read this type of book, then they have more doubts. The soul knows where to go after death regardless of doubt in life because the Divine takes care of it.

Q: What happens to our qualities after death?

MM: There are different planes for different qualities. Each quality goes to its plane.

Q: What becomes of the souls of those individuals who take their own life either because of great emotional and psychological pain, such as depression or because of enormous physical suffering as in terminally ill patients. Do such souls who have suffered so much in their earthly lives find peace in God's presence and light after death or do these souls occupy some other world separated from God?

MM: There are different types of reasons and purposes for suicide. If you are ill and there is no one to look after you, at this point if you commit suicide, it is different. If you have failure in your business and commit suicide, it is different. Some think that the world is not good and they cannot face the struggle and fight against their existence and they leave their body. When they leave their body, the suffering does not end with the end of the body.

The suffering continues even after death. They do not find peace after death.

Q: At the end of life, if your devotee does not remember you when leaving the body, what will happen?

MM: It is not possible to forget, if he is a real devotee.

Q: Is it possible for a human being after death to once again come back to life and write about their experience?

MM: No. When a person dies, it is not possible for him to come back again. Generally people mistake the vision for the reality. When one is unconscious and has the vision of death one can see the death, then when they again are conscious, they narrate the vision as an experience.

Q: My dog died. Where does it go? I lived 16 years with my dog.

MM: It goes to God.

Q: I am suffering from cancer. If I die where do I go?

MM: To God.

Q: Some people who are very sick commit suicide thinking that they will never get better and they do not want to live with the pain for the rest of their lives. So they commit suicide. Some say that is wrong and others accept it. May I know your opinion, Mother?

MM: If a person who is healthy but wants to avoid the problem of outside circumstances, commits suicide, it is bad, but for a person who is sick and cannot tolerate the pain and suffering throughout life, it is not as bad as the other. If there is someone to look after them with love and affection, then they do not think about dying because they have confidence that there is somebody who loves them and then these sick people feel that they can tolerate the pain because of this love and they can live for their loved ones. This is good.

Q: In many hospitals, people who are going to die in one or two weeks, are given large doses of tranquillisers. Is it good to be clear in consciousness or is it better to have tranquillisers?

MM: We cannot change the system. It is better to pray to God for the peaceful death of the patient.

అమ్మ

WORK

Q: My husband is a writer for a magazine. If the market for this magazine does not improve, he will lose his job. Now is the deadline. Mother, please help him. Otherwise we will be in great financial trouble and we will have nothing.

MM: Have faith in the Divine and pray to God. I will help.

> (Adilakshmi:) After a week she called and said that the Mother helped and she was very grateful and a miracle had happened. Now he still has the job.

Q: When money problems are important for example to pay the rent, the education of the children or our professional studies, can we hope for cosmic help?

MM: When there is an offering of a job, no matter if you like it or not, accept it and try it. This is a miracle. If you sit in the house and meditate, without trying to find a job, waiting for a miracle, then the miracle will never happen. So it is better to accept what comes and put it into practice, then comes the miracle.

Q: I have enough money and it is not necessary for me to work. What can I do?

MM: Work is essential. To maintain the physical body there must be some physical activity. When there is no physical work, then the body becomes weak and unhealthy.

Q: I have a problem in my work place, and I want to change my job. Will you help me?

MM: Wherever we may be, there is always some kind of problem. We cannot escape from the problem. It is better to stay in the same job. Try to be harmonious, friendly and loving with others and pray to God to dissolve the problem and also do japa. I will help you.

Q: What is the best attitude towards work?

MM: Work and serve others with love, not mechanically.

Q: I am a journalist and it is hard for the spiritual life. What to do?

MM: Do your journalism with the mind and your spiritual life with the heart.

Q: Mother, I am selling alcohol. Is it true that I am increasing my karma by doing this job?

MM: If we go on thinking that if we do this job, it is good and if we do another job, it is bad, then we cannot do anything in this life.

Q: I am involved in a legal case where a large company has a contract with the government. The company didn't act according to the contract. If the company loses the case, then there are many employees involved and they may have no jobs and their families will suffer. What is the best way to act?

MM: Nowadays, people are not truthful and honest. It is increasing day by day. It is better to control the dishonesty. Truth and honesty have their own values.

Q: I want to have a new job. Shall I leave the old job?

MM: First try to find a new job and when you are certain about it, then quit the old job.

Q: I have not enough to live on. I am a healer and astrologer.

MM: Do you have any other professional qualifications?

Q: Yes, I am a teacher.

MM: Try to find a job in your field and when you have free time, then you can practice these other two. First you must have a main job. Astrology and healing should be secondary jobs for you.

Q: Some healers advise me that my hands are good for healing. So I want to practice healing rather than do my job.

MM: When you have time, you can practice healing as a hobby but it is better to stick to your job.

Q: I bought a house and now I want to change my job.

MM: Don't change the job, do the same job.

Q: I took a case as a lawyer to help a friend rather than on the merits of the case. From the beginning I have had problems with this case. During the course of it, many times I tried to judge myself and see my own faults. It is difficult for me to proceed in this case and defend my client. What should my attitude be and how should I handle the case?

MM: As a lawyer, you should not involve yourself personally in the case. If you involve yourself in it, then you cannot proceed and you cannot defend. Leave yourself aside and try to defend your client. But on the other hand, for your growth, it is better to think of one's own mistakes and try to rectify them and offer them to God and also surrender to the Divine and pray for help to do good.

Q: In this case, the head of the community committed and involved others in sexual abuse. What is your feeling about it?

MM: I don't think that the mistake is only on one side but it is on both sides. I can agree that if it is child abuse, then the leader forced the children, and the mistake will be on one side. But here it is not so. He did not force anybody. They are all adults and all of them knew what they wanted. In this situation he or she speaks sweet words. He has the power and the other party also wants to have power. Here both play the game. We cannot just blame one person.

Q: They say that he deceived them.

MM: In this case, it depends on the level of feeling. Both wanted to fulfil their desires. The person who was involved came to know that it happened to others, and they had a breakdown. When they do not know what happened to others, until then, they feel safe and OK. As soon as they know that the same thing happened to others, then the problems arise. So, here we cannot blame the leader only.

Q: How to work with bad people? What should my attitude be towards them?

MM: With an open mind, work with the people but do not think that they are bad. Love them and try to help them to change, without duality of good or bad. There are no absolutely good ones and no absolutely bad ones.

Q: I am studying politics and I would like to work in business management but I have doubts about doing it.

MM: Don't doubt. If you like that work, you can try. I will help.

> (Adilakshmi:) With confidence in the Mother, he is now a very successful businessman.

Q: I have the possibility to teach arts at school. Can I do this profession?

MM: If you have the ability, then you can do it.

Q: I am an actor but not very successful.

MM: When you act, identify yourself with the part which you act. Begin your work with a prayer and offering and end your work with prayer and offering to God.

అమ్మ

FOOD

Q: Mother, is it necessary to be a vegetarian?

MM: Vegetarian or non-vegetarian is only a habit of the family background or the culture.

Q: Are you a vegetarian?

MM: Yes. But people should not follow what I eat but act according to their habits, customs, and culture. They can eat non-vegetarian food.

Q: I read how you comforted a dying kitten. I was touched by it and at the same time embarrassed when I read in the newspapers that in the Netherlands 60 million male chickens are killed yearly because they are economically of no interest. What is the best way to stop this? Not eating chicken or making laws or praying?

MM: Many things we cannot change. It is a habit and not a sin.

Q: I am overeating. Will you please help me?

MM: One must have self-control.

Q: Is eating meat good?

MM: As long as you have the desire and your body can digest it, you can eat meat.

Q: Why did you say that as long as I can digest it, I can eat meat? My grandmother is 90 years old and even now she eats meat and digests it.

MM: Is your grandmother doing yoga?

Q: When she was young she went to church. That is all.

MM: So for her the question doesn't arise.

Q: I heard that in India Brahmins and Vaisyas do not eat meat.

MM: Even in the family of Brahmins and Vaisyas some people eat meat but in the family of Kshatriyas and Sudras, some people do not eat meat. To eat or not to eat meat depends on the individual, not on caste.

అమ్మ

THE WORLD

Q: I read that your mission is bringing down the Light of Paramatman. Yet I see around us and inside people evil forces that do horrible things like killing and raping such as is now occurring in Bosnia. Except for your work, would the situation otherwise be worse, or is it only the spiritual result that counts and not the physical result in the visual world?

MM: The Light is helping in world crises. Otherwise, the evil forces would be even more dangerous.

Q: Now is a dangerous time. What is your position?

MM: The danger is there but do not emphasise the danger. If you emphasise danger, then the people will be nervous, depressed and hysterical. Instead it is better for people to stay calm, pray and do japa. For that reason alone, the world will be free from danger and crises.

Q: When there is a descent of Light, still there is suffering in the world. Is it going to change?

MM: There is always change. For instance, abolishing the Berlin Wall, black and white working together, high technology and so on.

Q: Is it possible to change the conditions of the world?

MM: Companies and governments should help change the conditions of the world.

Q: How is it possible?

MM: Through prayers.

Q: One of your devotees always emphasises that there is catastrophe or pain or suffering everywhere in the world. If we hear his talks, we are afraid to come to you and when we come and see you it is completely different. Why does he talk in this way?

MM: Because of his experience in his life, he projects it. He knows this experience. I have told him many times that it is not necessary to reach the Divine through suffering. But it is difficult for him to overcome it.

Q: I want to have Mother's help for world peace. I need the funds.

MM: If you want world peace, then pray to God or the Divine for peace. If you want help for your business, then I will help you.

Q: You have said we live in a crucial period for the earth. Is it crucial because large catastrophic events may occur or are major steps forward possible in our spiritual development.

MM: Many catastrophes have already happened. It is due in part to the lack of the global knowledge of the inventions of man. Man's whole concentration should be on the betterment of humanity, not for destruction. People have as their only aim power and money, nothing else. Human values are at a low ebb. Man must change his values and raise the moral and ethical levels. Then there is less danger. It is best and most important to turn towards the Divine.

Q: There is a strong rumour that there will be a Third World War in or before 1998, world population will be three-fourths wiped out and many nations will be destroyed by chemical, hydrogen and atom bombs. Then there will be peace after 2000. Then there will be destruction on the earth by earthquake, wind, storm, fire etc. What is your view towards these predictions?

MM: It is better to have positive thinking rather than negative.

Q: If it happens, how can people take precautions to survive?

MM: In all conditions, try to remember the Divine.

Q: I have spoken to people about not letting the pollution of our planet continue. I try to teach people that they live in the wrong way. Your work is directed towards a rapid transformation of this planet. Is this transformation possible without the active will of the people or should we first experience an environmental catastrophe, like a changing climate and flooding of the coasts, before people become more humble and more open to the Divine inspiration?

MM: Pollution is already here. People must have a strong will to change and prayer is the most important way to change it.

అమ్మ

INDIA

Q: People say that India is the spiritual leader of the world.

MM: Yes, it is.

Q: People in India are not modest, not honest and many are not spiritual, either. Most people give more value to worldly material life.

MM: The Mother Earth of India (Bhumata) is spiritual but not many of the people who are now living in India.

Q: Are Indians more advanced in spirituality than westerners?

MM: No.

> (Adilakshmi:) When I was in India in 1992, there was a drought and the earth was dry with cracks. I was unhappy with a heavy heart seeing the Mother Earth. I phoned the Mother for rain.

MM: Humanity is in such a condition that it is hard and difficult for Mother Earth to bear all this.

Adilakshmi: Even though the human beings are in such a condition, Ma, please help the earth. It is very hard for me to see Mother Earth in this condition.

(Adilakshmi:) The Mother was silent on the phone. Silence is one of the Mother's signals of help. Just as I put down the phone, the very next moment, the rain poured down heavily.

Q: In Indian philosophy, they say that there are four yugas: Krita Yuga, Treta Yuga, Dwapara Yuga, and Kali Yuga. Are they really existing?

MM: No. It is just like the names of the days, weeks, and months.

Q: In Ramayana. Sri Rama had two brothers called Lakshmana and Bharata. Both sacrificed their lives for Sri Rama. What is the difference between the two?

MM: Bharata had great aspiration and love for Sri Rama and with selflessness he ruled the country in the absence of Sri Rama. He adored with great devotion his brother. He adored the Shakti of Sri Rama whereas Lakshmana was in the presence of Shakti. So Bharata is greater than Lakshmana.

Q: Presently, I am living in Europe and my friends want to go to India. I am afraid that they have preconceived ideas about the beauty of India and all will be shattered by seeing the Indians. Is India truly spiritual?

MM: The earth (Bhumata) itself shows greatness. The land is great. The greatness is hidden inside the earth, not in the people outside.

Q: Should so much attention be paid to the past, i.e. the days of the Vedas?

MM: No.

అమ్మ

GENERAL

Q: What is Mother's general advice to people?

MM: People should live a normal life. Work normally and serve others who are in need.

Q: I am 60 years old and from my childhood until now I have been afraid of darkness. What shall I do?

MM: Believe that God exists and the Light will protect you, save you, and help you.

Q: I have great doubts about the usefulness of nuclear power for our society! Do you think that our society is ready for it? And how can we cope with the dangers of nuclear radiation as nuclear waste is produced already on a large scale in the world?

MM: This is man's creation and he has to bear the fruits of his action. Man must have a global idea of what he is inventing. Whatever may be his invention that must be constructive rather than destructive. Nuclear power is dangerous.

Q: Is there now or has there ever been human life or a similar level of life pattern on other planets in the cosmos? Have any past civilisations destroyed themselves leaving no trace of their existence?

MM: On the other planets there are beings but they are not like human beings.

Q: Have other beings existed on other planets from the beginning, and are they there even now?

MM: Yes.

Q: I have a project to help people. Would you kindly give the name?

Adilakshmi: Generally the Mother does not like to give names. You can name it what you want, The Mother's blessings will be there.

Q: I personally have the feeling that we should again become open to the work of all kinds of spiritual beings in nature, such as angels, mountain spirits, river goddess nymphs, elves, and gnomes and pay our respects to their work. We should restore the daily contact with these beings and should learn to co-operate with them. Do you agree and if so, how should we promote this?

MM: Prayer is the only solution. Through prayer all goodness can be achieved.

Q: Somebody told me that in my living room there is an evil force. Due to this force I have bad luck and also no sleep. What can I do?

MM: It is not true. Do not worry. I will help you.

Q: I hear some voices and see some visions. Is it good to act according to them.

MM: No. It is better to act according to common sense and live a practical and normal life.

Q: What is your opinion about Mother Theresa?

MM: She was a great saint.

Q: Does president Clinton have any more Paramatman Light than a drunken man?

MM: People elected him and they chose him to govern and he tries to rule in a better way. In this instance, it is not a question of more light or less light.

Q: Is there any light in a drunkard or a person who has bad habits?

MM: The person who smokes or drinks, because of the smell, it is inconvenient to other human beings, but there is light in them.

Q: Is it good to forgive them?

MM: Yes. God always gives them a chance to change.

Q: If they do not change, does God still give them a chance?

MM: God gives many chances and then God waits.

Q: Why does God give chances?

MM: Because God is an ocean of limitless patience. When a drunk person comes to his senses, he might realise that he made a mistake and asks God to pardon him. But once again he drinks and hurts his family or his wife. The whole family will suffer again and again if he doesn't change. Still there is a chance to change. His family or his friends can pray to God to help him.

Q: What will happen, if he cannot change and continues to drink?

MM: He is responsible for his actions and behaviour and must bear the consequences.

Q: Is Germany's spiritual atmosphere different from America's?

MM: Each country has its own spiritual atmosphere. For example, Thalheim is different from Limburg and Limburg is different from Frankfurt. It is the same with America.

Q: Is it the same as with different people having different spiritual paths?

MM: Yes. Each one has his or her own path.

Q: I want to change my name, can you give me a new name?

MM: There is no necessity to change your name. You change yourself within. That is important.

Q: Many developments are taking place in the biological sciences, for example in molecular engineering, DNA finger printing etc. What do you feel about the potential production of alternative life forms?

MM: In all things, there must be balance. In that there is imbalance.

Q: When an animal dies, for example a cat, does it come again as a cat or as a human being?

MM: It will be born as a cat.

Q: Never as a human being?

MM: It will take time.

Q: Will the human being always be the ultimate in God's creation?

MM: Always.

Q: I do not like rock music but my friend likes to play it. Is it good?

MM: If he likes to play it, he can play it.

Q: What is the best way to rest?

MM: Be peaceful and enjoy a good sleep.

Q: Nowadays, there is widespread abuse of parents by their children. Who is at fault?

MM: If you abuse your parents, look at yourself, not your parents.

Q: I want to help people. What should I do?

MM: First go deep within yourself and be peaceful and happy.

Q: What is the best way to go deep within?

MM: According to your age you have to detach yourself from worldly activities and pray for it. If you are in old age, it is better not to concentrate any more on worldly activities.

Q: My husband disappeared in 1949 while he was flying. There was no known air crash. I believe that he is alive. For me he may have disappeared into some other dimension, maybe into another world.

MM: If he is alive, then he must be on earth. Human beings with a physical body cannot enter the other worlds.

Q: Our hearts are with you and we want to come to see you all of the time. What shall we do?

MM: When hearts are here, bodies can come.

Q: Do you have any problems with the Germans?

MM: No. I have no problems with anybody. When people come and visit and pay for their hotels, then the local town people are grateful for my presence.

Q: Mother, I came many times having a wish to be fulfilled, but it is not fulfilled. Why?

MM: You came with too much expectation. So it is not fulfilled.

Q: I believe I can give light to change other human beings.

MM: By your vocabulary and your eloquence you can influence the minds of others but you cannot change their spiritual life. You cannot help their spiritual growth but you can influence their mental attitude towards spiritual growth. Due to your abilities, you influence more on their mental level.

Q: In January 1995, there is going to be a catastrophe in California and people are preparing for it.

MM: It is better to pray to the Divine or God that there should not be any catastrophe. It is better if people do not advertise about these things.

Q: What is your opinion about writers?

MM: In ancient times, writers wrote about their own experiences with intuition and sometimes with inspiration and also with some insight and dedication to the work like tapasya. If they wanted to write about holy places, they went by foot facing many dangers before reaching their destination. They needed more time and they had to face many difficulties because they did not have the transportation facilities that exist today. Because of this, even after many centuries, their writings are respected. But presently, the tendency for people is to write words without experience. Now people have an easy life and travel is easy. There are no hardships to visit holy places. It is like a fashion which changes so often, there is no deeper appreciation. Such writings will fade away like changing fashion. Today we read and tomorrow we will search for another.

(Adilakshmi:) One person came and said he would like to write a book about Mother. Then I asked the Mother about the interest of the person. The Mother asked, "How many times did he come for darshan?" When I said four or five times, the Mother said, "How can he write a book about me when he has spent so little of his life seeking the Divine." Then I told the person that "even people who have been living with a master or Guru for 20 or 30 years, are careful whether they write about their Master. Do you believe you can write a book after such a short time?"

Q: What about music?

MM: If we want to bring out the true depth of music, one must go deep into it. Go deep within to bring out real music. Real music comes from deep within.

Q: Is it necessary to hear Gandharva Veda music daily?

MM: No. If you have time and interest, then you can appreciate it.

Q: Should we feel guilty if the Divine has blessed us with material wealth?

MM: No.

Q: Has mankind become too preoccupied with its own creation and has mankind gone too far?

MM: Yes. Man must have balance. Man must try to remember the Divine as well as live in the world.

Q: By looking at your photo sometimes I see that your face is changing. Is it imagination?

MM: In the beginning some people said that they have seen my photos laughing, talking, and changing. If you see such things, you must be careful. We gradually learned that some of these people had psychological problems.

Q: Because of my personal life and my health, I cannot do what I want to do for mankind.

MM: When we are in public life and supported by the people, we are indebted to them. Sometimes we have to sacrifice our personal life for the public. When the public praises you, and it gives you happiness, it is OK. But when the public criticises you, then don't be depressed. Pray to the Divine to help you to improve the situation and ask for the strength to serve the public.

Q: Mother, we are informed that home deities are necessary. Is this true?

MM: If we have home deities, we must worship systematically and regularly, otherwise there are bad effects.

Q: What is the red spot on your forehead, Adilakshmi?

Adilakshmi: The red spot is called Bottu or Tilakam or Kumkum. In India, generally it is worn by a woman on the forehead between the eyebrows. It is not just decoration. It indicates that a woman has the shakti aspect of God. It indicates a woman who has not lost her husband. In a young woman it indicates that she is capable of marriage. This Bottu is made up of turmeric and lime. It is offered in worship to Shakti, chanting the names of Goddess Lakshmi, Durga, Saraswati, Maheshwari, Shakti, Kali etc., all forms of feminine Goddess, in puja. According to Agamas, the method to worship the Divine called 'Sri Chakra Puja' or ´Nava Abharana Puja´ (Nine Jewels) is done during the Full Moon (Poornima Day) and during the Navaratri Festival (Dassehra) on the Durga Puja Day. This is also called 'Kumkum'. It is a prasad offered in puja (worship) to the Shakti Deity, particularly for women to wear on their foreheads. It is sacred like Vibhuti. While ash is offered to Lord Shiva in Puja, so Kumkum and Vibhuti represent Shakti and Shiva to ward off all evils and to give the wearer blessings. It also represents a third eye with which developed souls or realised souls can see and experience the Divine.

It is also the place (between the eyebrows) for a kundalini chakra in the body (fifth chakra) and above it, the sixth chakra on the head. Therefore, it has a vital role for a woman, to receive the blessings of the Divine. In India, Kumkum is also worn by men who worship Shakti, Mahalakshmi, Durga, Saraswati, Maheshwari, etc.

It helps you and purifies you and prepares you to reach the Divine as it is sacred. The area between the eyebrows is also a seat of meditation.

Q: Was there anything in your earlier life that prepared you to live so close to the Mother?

Adilakshmi: I asked the Mother about your question. The Mother replied that there is no preparation to go to God. There is no need for preparation.

Q: Was it this way in your family?

Adilakshmi: Yes.

Q: This part of you, the part that loves God, was accepted and repeated in your family ?

Adilakshmi: Yes. I have an uncle who became a sannyasi and my grandmother was a devotee of Krishna.

Q: What is the place of the Divine in your life?

Adilakshmi: Without the Divine, there is nothing in life.

Q: As a child, what did you believe about God and Goddess?

Adilakshmi: Always, I felt God and Goddess as a family, just like my mother and the rest of the family.

Q: Even as a small child this was so?

Adilakshmi: Yes. Always.

Q: How does doubt arise in you?

Adilakshmi: What kind of doubt do you mean?

Q: Well, small doubts, the feeling of unworthiness or fearful or when there is a crisis etc.

Adilakshmi: I just ask the Mother for help.

Q: Is there no sense of unworthiness or fear for you? No doubt about God?

Adilakshmi: No. Children have no fear with the love of their mother. I always feel God as a family member. It is a reality for me. I have full confidence that God exists. That's why I left home with nothing to find Mother in everything.

అమ్మ

SRI AUROBINDO RESEARCH ACADEMY

(Adilakshmi:) From the beginning until now, Mother's wisdom keeps me spellbound. When She was a teenager, people in the Sri Aurobindo Ashram who lived with Sri Aurobindo and Sweet Mother wished to meet the Mother. These people were the intellectual leaders of the Ashram. In 1978, the Mother, Mr. Reddy and myself attended a meeting with those leaders. They asked the Mother many questions about different subjects. The Mother's answers were always precise and touched the heart and satisfied the intellect of the Ashram leaders.

After this meeting, some people came to the Mother and asked Her advice for their personal spiritual growth. They were surprised to hear the same advice for their growth which was given to them by Sri Aurobindo and Sweet Mother.

At the same time in 1978, UNI, an Indian Government newspaper wrote about the Mother's Divinity throughout India.

Here are some of the answers that the Mother gave in Sri Aurobindo Ashram:

Q: Do you feel the presence of Sweet Mother and Sri Aurobindo always or do you feel that they appear before you on occasion?

MM: Always.

Q: How do you know that they are Sweet Mother and Sri Aurobindo?

MM: They introduced themselves to me.

Q: Do you see them always or do you feel them?

MM: Always I see them.

Q: What are their forms?

MM: They resemble their physical forms, but they are full of energy and illumination, which takes different forms.

Q: What does Sri Aurobindo look like?

MM: He is serene and tranquil like a mountain and rarely smiles.

Q: What is the difference between Paramatman and Nirvana?

MM: Paramatman is full of light and Nirvana is a portion of it.

Q: What shall we do when people speak out against Sri Aurobindo?

MM: You offer it to Sri Aurobindo.

Q: When people come and offer their pranam to the Samadhi, how do Sweet Mother and Sri Aurobindo respond to them?

MM: They smile and bless them.

Q: Do you want to be a yogi or a great person.

MM: No.

Q: Do you want to change some particular persons or the world?

MM: The world.

Q: Why do you not get rid of all your physical troubles by higher forces?

MM: When I am in supramental consciousness I forget about them.

Q: Do you find any difference between before and after the experience of the Supramental?

MM: Yes. there is a great difference.

Q: What do you feel when the supramental forces descend?

MM: The body becomes light, instead of heavy. Supermind is full of light, knowledge, peace, power, and bliss.

Q: Have you seen any ashramites in the supramental world?

MM: I have seen some.

Q: Sweet Mother said that there is a building in the subtle world where Sri Aurobindo resides. Mother used to go there. Have you seen that building?

MM: Yes.

Q: By thinking are you answering?

MM: No. It is not possible to speak with the mind. I see things and tell about them.

Q: After the descent of the Supermind you say that you know everything. What does this mean?

MM: I am full of knowledge.

Q: People are saying that Sweet Mother left her body because she could not finish her work. Is it true?

MM: No. It is not true. Sweet Mother left her body because it was tired. She is still continuing her work. When the Mother was in her physical body how do you know what work the Mother was doing?

Q: Nowadays there are more difficulties both in the Ashram and outside. What is your opinion as to why such difficulties are taking place?

MM: Because there is no complete surrender.

Q: Can you give Light, Knowledge, Bliss, and Peace to others.

MM: If they are ready to receive then I can give to them.

Q: Will you tell us what level of consciousness people have obtained?

MM: No.

Q: Will Sweet Mother's and Sri Aurobindo´s work be done?

MM: Yes. Surely.

Q: Will the work be done in the Ashram?

MM: Everywhere, outside also. Light is descending always.

Q: In the world?

MM: Yes, in the world, in the Ashram, everywhere.

Q: When will the work be done?

MM: Sri Aurobindo and the Mother are always working.

Q: What do you expect in the world?

MM: All suffering should be removed. All should be changed into something fine, enlightened. The Light is always descending.

అమ్మ

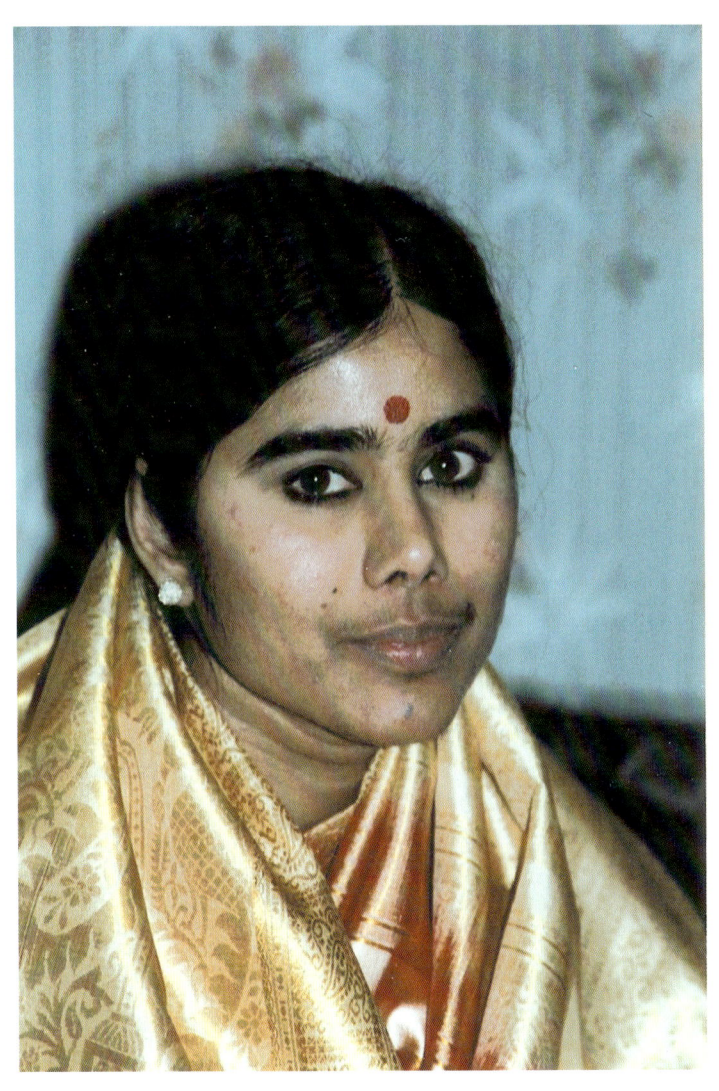

Thalheim, Germany 1996

NAMES AND TERMS

Absolute: The Supreme Divine Being.
Adiparashakti and Adishakti: The original Shakti. The Supreme Mother.
Advaita: The philosophy of non-dualism.
Agni Deva: God of Fire.
Amavasya: New Moon.
Amma, in Telugu అమ్మ: Mother.
Angel: Messenger from God (particularly in Christian belief).
Avadhuta: A realised soul. A person identified with the Supreme. An ascetic who has abandoned all worldly bondage.
Avatar: An incarnation of the Divine on earth.
Brahma: The Creator.
Brahmin: Member of the priestly caste. There are four castes (Brahmins, Kshatriyas, Vaishyas, and Shudras) in India.
Darshan: Self-revelation of the deity to the devotee.
Deva: God.
Dharma: Duty, Virtue, Right, a rule or a principle.
Divine: The Supreme Self.
Divine Mother: The Supreme Mother.
Dowry: In Indian tradition, the father of the bride has to give property or money to the husband.

Durga: The conquering and protecting aspects of the Universal Mother.
Ganapati: The power that removes obstacles by the force of Knowledge.
Gangabhavani: Goddess of Water.
Gita: Bhagavad Gita ("The Song of God"). It is a mystical poem which contains 18 chapters with unique combination of philosophy, poetry, and mysticism.
Gods and Goddesses: The personalities or powers put forth by the Divine.
Guru: A spiritual Master or teacher.
Homa: A burnt offering.
Ishwara: The Lord. Also a name for Shiva.
Jivanmukta: One who has become emancipated from all desires. A man who is in the world but not of the world. Literally means 'liberated while living'.
Jnani: A follower of the path of knowledge.
Jyotish: Astrology.
Karunamayi: Epitome of Compassion, full of Mercy.
Krishna: An incarnation of Vishnu.
Lakshmi: Goddess of Supreme Love and Delight.
Maha: Great.
Mahakali: Goddess of Force and Strength.
Mahalakshmi: See Lakshmi.

Maharishi: Great Seer.
Mahasaraswati: See Saraswati.
Maheshwari: Goddess of supreme Knowledge.
Nirguna Parabrahman: Pure Consciousness without attributes.
Nirvana: The liberated condition of the being.
Paramatman: The Supreme Self, the Absolute, the Supreme Divine Being.
Parvati: Spouse of Shiva.
Premamayi: Epitome of Love.
Puja: Ceremony of gratitude to the master or to a deity.
Pujari: Priest in the temple.
Pundit: Scholar.
Rama: A divine incarnation.
Ramayana: An epic poem of the Hindus, recording the adventures of Rama (who is an incarnation of Vishnu), the son of Dasaradha, brother of Lakshmana and Bharata, husband of Sita.
Rishi: A seer.
Sadhana: Spiritual practice and self-discipline.
Samadhi: A sacred tomb for the preservation of a holy body after death. Also a state of union with the Divine.
Saraswati: Goddess of Learning and Perfection.
Shakti: Energy and power.
Shiva: Another name for Ishwara.

Siddhi: The fruit of sadhana.

Sikh: A follower of Sikhism, a religion started by Guru Nanak.

Sri Aurobindo: The greatest Indian yogi and philosopher of modern times. He lived most of his yogic life in Pondicherry, in French India. He was the author of several metaphysical masterpieces, the greatest of which is *The Life Divine*. He was also a great poet and wrote an epic poem, *Savitri*. The yoga of Sri Aurobindo which is indebted to traditional Indian yogas, transcends their limitations. It is an Integral Yoga, a yoga that does not deny or flee life as illusion, but desires the complete and radical transformation of life on earth. Sri Aurobindo's task was to call down into the consciousness of the earth the Supramental Light, that would enable the transformation of life into the Divine Life, and to make humanity aware of that Light and open to it.

Supramental: The plane of consciousness above the Overmind.

Sweet Mother: Sri Aurobindo's Shakti or Divine Partner in the work of transformation. A French woman, She lived in Pondicherry and began the Ashram there. She is worshipped as an Incarnation of the Divine Mother by Her devotees. It was Sweet Mother's task to bring down the

Supramental Light into the consciousness of the earth and She did so in 1956, thus making the transformation certain. She left her body in 1973 at the age of ninety-five.

Tapasya: Practice of Yoga.

Veda: The earliest literature of the Indians. There are four Vedas.

Vibhuti: An incarnation that comes for a certain, specific work, more related to the world. Also sacred ash.

Vishnu: The Protector, the Lord of Protection.

Yagna: Vedic sacrifice.

Yashoda and Nanda: Foster parents of Lord Krishna.

Yoga: Union with the Divine.

Yogi: One who attains the union with the Divine with spiritual endeavour and discipline.

Yuga: An age. There are four yugas.

అమ్మ

DARSHAN INFORMATION

Mother Meera gives 4 Darshans every week.
Friday, Saturday, Sunday and Monday evening at 7 pm (19:00 hrs German time). Check-in at 6:15 pm (18:15 hrs).

Darshan reservations: 7 days a week 10 am - 5 pm (10 - 17 hrs German time).
Tel: +49 (0) 6436 / 91050 & 91051 & 2305, Fax 2361.

Fax-on-Demand: You may download the directions.
Fax +49 (0) 6436 / 2361, +49 (0) 6432 / 508853.

Darshan is free, no payment is required.
Reservations are required and can only be made by telephone. Please call several weeks in advance. Visitors should be able to sit quietly for two hours and should have stable enough health to be able to attend the darshan without disturbance. Children are not allowed to come – they receive Mother's Blessings through their parents. Come dressed normally, with washed hair and wear clean socks.

Questions to Mother: through Adilakshmi or others by telephone every Fri, Sat, Sun and Mon 4 pm - 5 pm (16 - 17 hrs German time). Tel. +49 (0) 6432 / 508833. All letters to Mother should be in English or German.

Darshan address:
Mother Meera's Home
Schloss Schaumburg
65558 Balduinstein
Germany

Postal address:
Mother Meera
Oberdorf 4a
65599 Dornburg-Thalheim
Germany

The following **books** are available:
Answers, Part 1 by Mother Meera
Answers, Part 2 by Mother Meera
The Mother by Adilakshmi
Bringing Down the Light – Paintings by Mother Meera in three languages (English, German and French).

Photos of Mother Meera in passport size, 9x13 cm, 13x18 cm and 20x30 cm are also available.

The books and photos can be ordered from:
Mother Meera Home Colorado
P.O.Box 3453
Boulder, CO 80307-3453
email: mothermeerahomecolorado@gmail.com
Mother Meera Ashram - Midwest
P.O.Box 802458
Chicago, IL 60680-2458
email: information@mothermeeraashram-midwest.org
Mother Meera Ashram - Midwest
P.O.Box 2183
Fairfield, IA 52556
email: information@mothermeeraashram-midwest.org

Directions to Mother Meera's Darshan

Travel by aeroplane: Fly into Frankfurt Airport, Hahn or Köln/Bonn.
By train from Frankfurt airport to Limburg: Tickets to Limburg/Balduinstein at the Travel Center or at the ticket machine at Terminal **1** below the airport section **B**.
1) **S**-Bahn: Airport – Frankfurt Main Station 2) Frankfurt –

Limburg/Lahn (possible change in Niedernhausen) 3) In Limburg change to local train or taxi and travel to Balduinstein or your destination.

Or direct train (**ICE**, Inter City Express) from Frankfurt Airport (Fernbahnhof) to Limburg-Süd and then via taxi or local train to Balduinstein or your destination (you need to take the shuttlebus from Limburg-Süd to Limburg main station if you want to continue by local train). This connection is much faster but more expensive.

By train from other directions: Train Giessen-Limburg-Koblenz. Balduinstein is the 3rd station after Limburg. You may walk from Balduinstein to Schaumburg. But be aware: it is a 30 min. walk uphill and you need a torch and good shoes. There are no buses or trains to Schaumburg.

By car: To rent a car it is advisable to negotiate the price before leaving home.

From Frankfurt airport to Schaumburg (1 hour app.) follow signs for A3 (Autobahn 3) to Wiesbaden and then Köln (Cologne).

From Frankfurt City follow signs for A66 to Wiesbaden, then A3 to Köln.

1) Leave A3 at Exit Limburg-Süd>Limburg 2) After tunnel turn left to B54 Bad Schwalbach/Diez. 3) In Diez turn left to B54>Bad Schwalbach/Katzenelnbogen. 4) After 1,5 km turn right to Katzenelnbogen/Birlenbach. 5) After Birlenbach turn right in the curve (concrete divider) to Balduinstein/Schaumburg. The castle appears on your left after 1 km.

From Cologne (Köln): Leave A3 at Exit 41 Diez/Nassau. Take a right turn twice to Nassau/Eppenrod. Follow signs Hirschberg > Langenscheid > Balduinstein > Schaumburg.

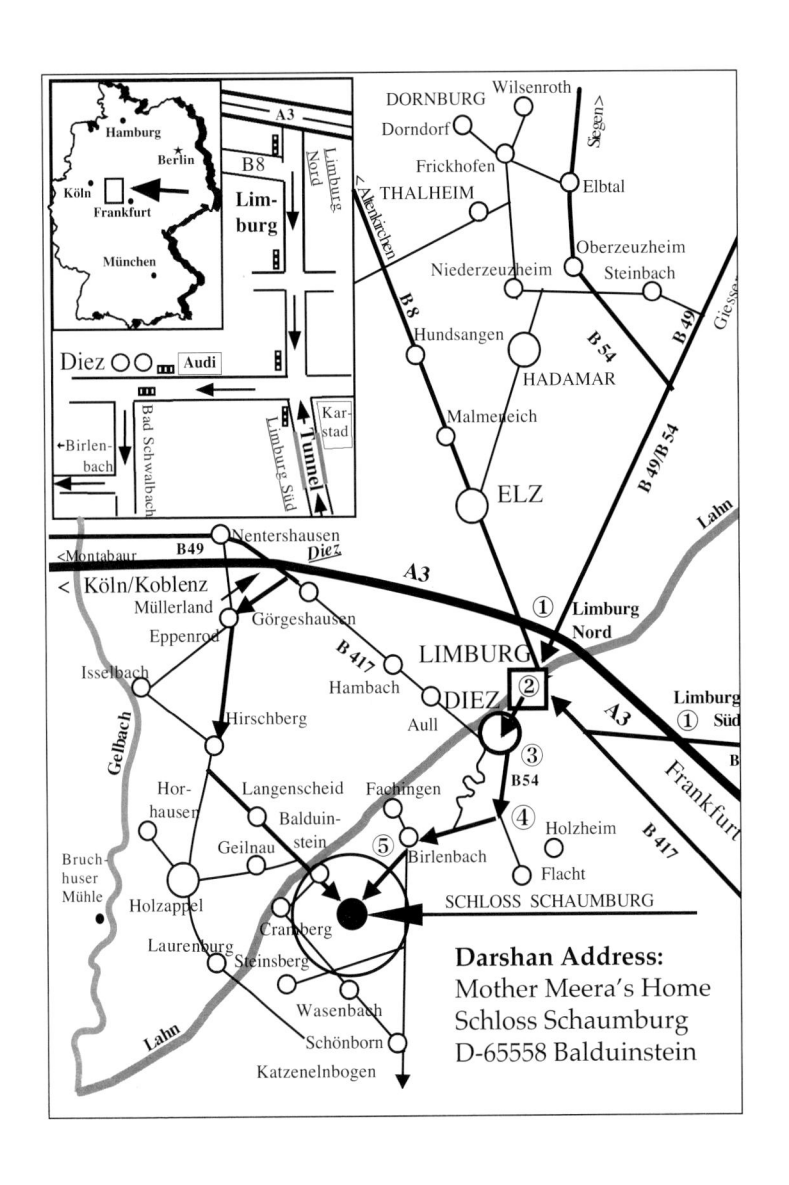

Darshan Address:
Mother Meera's Home
Schloss Schaumburg
D-65558 Balduinstein